Dear Fathe

Dear Father Michael

MICHAEL BUCKLEY

DARTON·LONGMAN + TODD

First published in 1996 by
Darton, Longman and Todd Ltd
1 Spencer Court
140–142 Wandsworth High Street
London SW18 4JJ

ISBN 0–232–52196–4

A catalogue record for this book is available
from the British Library

Designed by Sandie Boccacci
Phototypeset in 10/12¾pt Times by Intype London Ltd
Printed and bound in Great Britain by
Redwood Books, Trowbridge, Wiltshire.

Foreword

Most of us have reached some moment or another in our lives that we considered a crisis – the loss of a loved one, of our health, our job, our faith in God, or some problem that seemed an unbearable agony. And when we came crashing to the edges of that despair, most of us found too that it was a desperately lonely place, where few either understood or cared what we were going through.

When I began editing the *Universe*, I vividly remember my first reaction to the 'Dear Father Michael' page: it appeared somewhere between the news and the television reviews, a harmless blending of prayer and problems that fitted snugly into the features section of an otherwise news-hungry Catholic paper.

As I got to know Father Michael, and the countless people who wrote to him every week, I changed my views about where the real news was coming from: of course we reported world events, national events, the complexities of theology and the great moral dilemmas that society throws at us. But I kept coming back to Father Michael's page, to its ordinary – but, equally, extraordinary – people; and I discovered that the Catholic Church is not a collection of textbooks and lofty theology, but a great human family of all the world and its hopes, its fears and its fragile dreams.

I learnt too that lasting happiness comes not from material things, from prescriptions or a pill packet, but from prayer and sharing. I suppose I've acquired those two words from Father Michael; they were always hanging around in my vocabulary, but when I use them now they have a sense of meaning and energy that no textbook could have taught me. Fr Michael will tell you that prayer and sharing are the essence of his healing ministry, but they are also the very essence of Christianity itself.

If I have dreams of a faith that is at once beside a fishing boat in Galilee, and in the heart of our modern cities, it is that image of Christian praying and sharing. This selection of prayers and problems from the *Universe*'s 'Dear Father Michael' page is the Church that I came looking for, the story of a great multitude of people sharing their lives, and the gentle priest who ministers to them.

JOE KELLY
Editor of the *Universe*

Introduction

People are hurting deep inside. They have all sorts of problems in their lives with which they cannot cope. They need someone in whom they can confide; someone whom they regard as a special friend. Although their lives seem divorced from the obligatory Sunday Mass, they look to the Church for help.

In my attempts to help people, I soon found that their needs were deeper than I had encountered in ordinary parish life. I realised that if I were to be able to help, then I had to identify with their pain. It was this identification with people's problems which propelled me into the healing ministry. I founded El Shaddai, a Christian movement for inner healing, and travelled the country holding healing services. The need was awesome, and I knew immediately that this is where I belonged, and where people were hurting. I encouraged them to write to me and I have spent many years answering their letters, and letting them know through my books and tapes that they are not alone. I wanted to become their dear friend.

I was given a golden opportunity by the *Universe* to devote a whole page of their weekly paper to answering the problems people were facing in their everyday lives. The response was beyond my wildest dreams. The outreach to thousands every week has become one of the main platforms of my healing ministry. The letters, while remaining anonymous, speak to many who can identify with the pain and problems of the person who asks for help. They see themselves in the 'other person' with whom they can identify. In my replies I enclose a prayer card which invites them to pray for all those who are hurting and need help. Every day thousands of people say the El Shaddai prayer. They feel part of our Christian family.

This book is a very small selection of the letters I have received, and were used over the past year in the *Universe*. I am grateful to the staff who have supported my ministry, and who gave me this very special Christian outreach to my brothers and sisters suffering in our world. I thank in particular Denis Lane, Joe Kelly and Gary Denning for the sensitive way in which the 'Dear Father Michael' page is produced. The El Shaddai secretaries, Rose Wainwright and Celia Luker, have tackled a mountain of correspondence with extreme confidentiality and efficiency stamped with a personal approach. Morag Reeve of Darton, Longman and Todd was, as always, an encourager and a spur to the compilation of this book. The sharing by Oonagh Watters was such that without it this healing venture would never have seen the light of day. No praise is too great for her. Finally, I thank God for the people I have met on the road whose faith, despite all their problems, is a source of healing for me. They have become my dear friends.

MICHAEL BUCKLEY
August 1996

Things are going from bad to worse

I'm a pessimist. I look back over the past year. It has not been a good year for the Church or the country. When, and how, is the slide going to stop?

KEVIN

No, it has not been an excitingly brilliant year. We have suffered a great deal in the Church. I hope we have learned from our mistakes. They should help us to be more courageous and not tempt us to withdraw into a more 'secure' position. We are not meant to be a 'safety-first' organisation. If we have leadership problems, perhaps it is because we are not allowing ourselves to be more open to the challenge of the Gospel. We have to take risks. This is not because we are foolhardy but because we are optimists.

If we lived out our lives as optimists, then the Second Vatican Council which ended thirty years ago would have been absorbed into every aspect of our parish life long ago. But sadly this is not so. We are more than half way through the Decade of Evangelism, and where are the strikingly visible results?

Kevin, you and I are responsible for this apathy if we are pessimists who live in the dug-out trenches of the past. The world has moved on and we must move challenging it by the vision and energy within ourselves.

I want to change the world. Don't you? If I can't, then at least I'm never going to stop trying to change *my* world. Together we can make the Church and country a better, more vital place. At least we can try. Don't be a pessimist. This is to accept failure and defeat. We are never beaten.

❦ **Lord**, teach me to look on the bright side of everything so that even the darkest cloud has a silver lining. Let me turn my face towards your radiance so that I may reflect your light and hope which will lift people up to believe that in all things you are changing our world to make it a better place in which to live.

Who is a healer?

I have been to healers for my arthritis. I felt better for a while but then the effects wore off and I feel worse now because my hopes were misplaced. You constantly write about healing. What do you mean by healing?

JILL

Healing is a very much misused and misunderstood word. People who set themselves up as 'healers' claim to have special psychic powers or forces of energy which heal people of all sorts of illnesses. 'Spiritual' healing is one of the fastest growing professions today. This can damage the whole cause and concept of Christian healing.

As Christians we believe, Jill, that only God our Father can heal us through his Son Jesus Christ. Christ is our healer. I cannot heal by my own powers but Christ uses me and others as ministers of his healing so that people can live a fuller and better life as human persons and Christians. All I can do is to pray in faith that God in his love will free us from all those things which hurt and hinder us because we live in a sinful world.

I am not special in an exclusive sense that I am the only minister of healing. I am there for the people, for the Christian church, so that ultimately glory and praise is given to God. The danger is when people begin to treat you as if you had unique magic powers.

If anyone tells you he is a healer, Jill, then watch out. There are all sorts of counterfeit healers around. Remember,

2

only Christ heals. When you lose sight of that you are entering the area of superstition and magic where Christ does not live.

All of us, priests and people need to study, understand and experience Christian healing. If we don't then all sorts of false theories and practices will mushroom and people will be damaged. It is to remedy this gap in Church practice that I have devoted my life to Christian healing. I never give people false hope. To do so would cause untold harm. However, I do encourage people to turn to Christ in their pain. He will never disappoint them. He came on earth to heal people. He heals today through you and me.

❦ LORD JESUS, you walked our earth aware of the sadness around you. People were hungry, not only for bread, but because of something deep inside which troubled their spirit and cast them down. You met their every need because this is what your Father wanted you to do. Be with me today, Lord, as I go out to meet my wounded brothers and sisters. It is your touch alone, Lord, which heals, it is you they need not me. Live in me, Lord, so that when I meet them they will know it is you living in me which heals them and brings them hope.

Now for the Good News

Thank God for El Shaddai and the inner healing ministry. It has transformed my life. Here is my story and it is really 'good news'.

All my life until I went to an inner healing service I felt that I was living an unreal life. I did not feel good in myself because I was not being true to the person I knew existed deep inside me. I never got to know the real 'me' because those around me never encouraged me to be myself. I was always the person other people wanted me to be. For my father, I was 'a chip off

3

the old block'. I had to be like him in all I said and did if I was to gain his approval. Real love never entered into it. It was the same with my teachers at school. I conformed because this was the easiest, and for me the only way out. It was the same with my 'friends' at school. I was part of a gang, a group, where the group meant conforming with certain sorts of behaviour. I was one of them, never myself. I now know I allowed myself to be manipulated.

Naturally, I treated my wife and children in the same way. They too had to conform to my image of them, and why not? I had to, so why shouldn't they? Then things started to go wrong. When my children became adolescents they started questioning my set of values. I had a rebellious family on my hands and I couldn't cope. In desperation, rather than hope, I came to an El Shaddai healing service. You spoke of the uniqueness of each individual and that if we couldn't be ourselves we were a nobody. You spoke of the need for parents to encourage their children to be themselves. After the service when I came home I told the children all about it and how I suffered from my father. 'But Dad', said the eldest, 'you are like that with us.' It went home like a dagger to my heart. He was right. I resolved there and then to change, but it was easier said than done. All I had ever known rebelled against my new attitude.

I came to many more healing services. I needed to because old habits die slowly. Today, four years later, I can honestly say I have a very good relationship with my wife and children. We are partners in our family. I have found myself at long last. I don't like everything I've found, but I am glad for the discovery. My faith has deepened in an extraordinary way and I love myself because I know God loves me, warts and all. He loves and wants me to be myself.

SIMON

❦ **FATHER**, you have made each one of us unique, and by your love you encourage us to be ourselves. Even though we

4

live in a family, like any parent, you love us in our differences. Each of us in our own way finds a unique response from you as we reflect your love. I thank you for my parents and family who wanted me to be different, and I bless you that we were a united rather than a uniform family. You bound us closely together by light strings of love rather than unbending rules of discipline. In my freedom to be myself, I found you, my leader and friend, who is my true freedom and guide. I pray for parents who find it difficult to express their love for their children in their own home because they never experienced it themselves when they were young. I thank you for the many parents who were healed of the effects of their childhood and gave to their children the warmth and love necessary for their growth.

I cannot stop grieving

I was blessed with a most wonderful caring husband who died seven years ago. I just cannot stop grieving. I cry every day and in my heart I feel I am hurting myself and my family. Am I doing wrong because I feel unable to cope with my grief?

JESSICA

It is good to grieve. Jesus said 'Blessed are those who mourn they shall be comforted' (Matthew 5:4). The gift of tears for someone we have shared our lives with is very necessary if we are to grow through our pain. But, Jessica, we have to *grow* through it. We cannot stand still. 'We do not grieve as others do who have no hope' (Thessalonians 4:13). You will see your beloved husband again because you believe in the resurrection. He would not have you grieve endlessly. He is part of the living Church, who has gone beyond death into life which has no end. Our faith is all about *life not death*.

I appreciate how you feel but if your grief is hurting you and your family then it cannot be right. Perhaps there is a touch of selfishness in it. Why not thank God for the love you shared with your husband when he was alive and be with him in spirit so that you can carry on with living. 'Let the dead bury their dead', said the Lord (Matthew 8:22), and this is what we all have to do when there is a temporary parting of the ways. But it is only temporary. You will see your husband again and there will be no more parting or mourning or tears (Revelations 21:4).

❦ JESUS, when you wept over the death of Lazarus you showed us the value of grieving at the passing of a loved one. You told us that those who grieve would be comforted. I thank you for the gift of tears which you gave me and which released my grief at the deaths of my parents, brother and sisters, and loved ones. The tears were for my healing. They were a mixture of sorrow and joy; sorrow because I was physically separated from those I loved, and joy because of my strong belief that we would meet again, never to part. I thank you that you said of yourself, 'I am the resurrection and the life. He who believes in me will never die.' The memory of your promise has lightened the burden of sorrow when I grieve. Comfort all those who as yet have not found solace in their distress and give them the gift of tears which will be a mixture not only of sorrow, but also of hope.

Living the Gospel today

We are always being told in my church about life after *death but I rarely hear a sermon about life* before *death. Shouldn't we be hearing about everyday life's problems, and how we should face up to them, as well as talking about eternity? I want to hear sermons on how I can live my life now. Am I wrong?*

JIMMY

6

Of course there is life *before* death. This is what the Christian Gospel is all about. Jesus came that we might have life and have it to the full (John 10:10). This means life in this world as well as the next. To concentrate on death and not on life is contrary to the emphasis Christ gave to living life to the full. Death is only a hiccup between this life and the next. The Gospel is about life not death. A friend of my age told me last week he had given up on this world and was preparing for eternity. That is not how I live. Every day in this life is to be lived to the full. It is the best and only Christian way to prepare for heaven. I am alive today in today's world.

I agree with you, Jimmy. I want to hear about what my Christian attitude should be to everything that is happening in the world round me. I have to live in this world today. This is where I discover the Gospel and see it come alive in my situation. Christ's reaction to events during his life on earth is my yardstick. For example, when I read my daily newspaper I wonder how Christ would react. He is my 'stop press' as I live in my world moment by moment. He is the '*good news*' come alive in me. This is what living the Gospel means. It is Christ alive today in my life.

❦ HOLY SPIRIT, I come alive when I hear your Gospel preached in church in a living meaningful way. Your message is of life not death. You teach me how to live in my world. Nothing is outside the scope of your message. Teach me to live my life to the full, so that every aspect of it is shot through with the brilliance of your resurrection. May I never withdraw from the world except to find you in prayer and refreshed by you may I go back to people reflecting your love and care for them.

I'm afraid of my operation

In four weeks' time I have to undergo a serious operation and I am scared. Will I survive? Will it be successful? I am fifty-seven and I have never been in hospital before. What should I do to get rid of this awful fear?

RACHEL

The worst thing that could happen to you now is to be afraid. Fear affects your body, your emotions and is the worst possible preparation for any operation. Recently, a joint statement published by the Board of Doctors and Psychiatrists in this country highlighted the effects of stress in people. It *causes* physical and psychological disorders. They emphasise the need for people to be at peace within themselves. This is one of our main aims in the El Shaddai Inner Healing Movement. We try to make people aware of the need for inner peace. As Christians we see this peace as Christ's very precious gift to his followers.

Rachel, trust God with the outcome of this operation. Pray for skill on behalf of the doctors and nurses who will be looking after you. Pray, too, for your own peace of mind. The operation is your cross, and, like Jesus, you leave the outcome to God your loving Father. He will see you through. We will pray for you as well. You will grow through this operation as a Christian person. Do not be afraid. All will be well when you are at peace within yourself.

❦ **SPIRIT OF HEALING AND WHOLENESS**, I commit all that I am, my body, emotions and spirit to your tender care. I thank you for doctors, nurses and all those who have care of the sick. Bless their skills and in trusting them, may I show my total commitment and trust to you. May I never lose this trust which is the source of my inner peace. Bless all those who today will have a surgical operation so that they will be composed and peaceful, secure in your love for them that all will be well.

Now for the Good News

I came with my mum and my brother to two of your healing Masses, but I don't know if you will remember me. My name is Jimmy and I am 13. I was born with glaucoma and have quite poor eyesight. I have had lots of operations and have regular checkups at the hospital.

When I was a baby, my parents were told that I would never see, but everybody prayed that I would. Mum and Dad took me to the hospital and we believe a miracle happened because the doctors said I would have useful vision.

I am doing well, and go to a normal school, where I get lots of help and support from my teachers and my friends. My condition is stable and must remain that way so I lose no more vision. Every night I ask Jesus to cure my eyes because I know he can. If he doesn't cure them I pray that my vision doesn't get any worse so I can be safe and do normal things. Please remember me in your prayers and ask Jesus to look after me always.

LOVE FROM JIMMY

❦ **LORD JESUS**, the age of miracles is never past for you. You heal people today as truly as you did when you walked the roads of Galilee. The blind called on you then that you might restore their sight so that they could see again. I ask you now, Lord, to renew my faith in you and your loving Father so that I might see again with the eyes of faith the beauty of the simple love I once had for you as a child. Give me back my child's eyes and renew my faith so that I might look on you again as someone who never stops loving and healing me.

I want to share my faith

I really appreciate my faith but I can't seem to share it with my fellow parishioners. Our Sunday Mass is so mechanical and lifeless. Will ordinary Sunday services ever change?

FRANK

We all need to experience a living faith. This is why we come to Sunday Mass in which we are nourished so that we can live out the rest of the week in our world. You say you are not being fed in this way and I feel so sorry for you. Mass should heal us. In a true sense every Mass is a healing Mass, but I too have experienced Masses where the atmosphere is rather wooden and dry. I have been on the other side of the altar, and I have suffered from the apathy of a dead congregation. Not all churches are like that, but many are.

What we all need, priests and people, is to see Mass as a living challenge to our life and world. The Gospel challenges us, or it should. If it does not, then something has gone drastically wrong. If a Mass is to heal then it must flow from a deep faith. Faith is not only about belief in doctrine, but in how we live our daily lives. *It is word and deed.* We need to come to Mass in a spirit of expectancy and hope. Mass is not all rubrics and liturgical actions. These are only the packaging. The real message is that in Mass we, priests and people, encounter a living Christ who encourages us to live by the light of his resurrection. Stay alive in your church, Frank, and keep the others awake and alive as well. We need living vibrant Christian communities if we are to be true to the Gospel.

❦ **SPIRIT OF THE LIVING GOD**, I praise you that each day you renew in me the message of Jesus Christ so that I find in it the great challenge to my life. You give inspiration to the acts of worship in your Church in which I share so that they nourish me, and give me an experience of your living presence. Without your Spirit within me, I could never truly worship you in word or action because these would not penetrate the real me. I would never come to realise what prayer really means unless you pray in me, and give my life meaning in all that I say and do. Be with everyone today in their worship together. Bring them alive with your Spirit so that they thrill to the message of Jesus our Lord and Master.

What happens when I'm gone?

I have been diagnosed as having terminal cancer, with six months to live. I am terrified although I try to be strong and positive, especially when my priest comes with my weekly Holy Communion. My main concern is for my son, trapped in an unfortunate marriage, a lapsed Catholic with a lapsed Catholic wife. We are so close, what will he do? He is devastated now. I am 76 and he 46, but when I have gone what will sustain him? All we can do is pray with faith and courage, but it's hard and my hope and trust are sorely tried.

ELIZABETH

I appreciate your anxiety for your son's future when you are gone, but you are alive now and the important thing is to make the most of each day. The best way to help your son is to show him that you love him. Share with him, and the fact that you know how important each day is will make you all the keener to live it to the full.

You will not be able to do this if you worry. A worried person is a divided person. Be at peace within yourself. God will look after your son just as he looked after you. That is why we call him Father. Who knows how long your life will be? God knows best. You give your life and that of your son to his tender care and all will be well.

Let me tell you a story that will help you. Many years ago I met Mary whose case is very similar to yours. I showed her how to discover inner peace by trusting God. She died without ever knowing what the future held for her son. He was still lapsed when she died. Six months afterwards I met him at a healing service. He was back right in the heart of the Church. I asked him how it came about. 'In a strange way', he said, 'I knew how much my mother's faith meant to her and how she longed for me to return to the practice of my religion. Even though I made no response she loved me in a way which was very deep and beautiful. If her faith meant that much to my mother, I felt I had to do something about it in my own life. I suppose that is why I came back home to my mother and her Church.'

So Elizabeth, don't worry. The stray come home because the Shepherd looks after them all the time, even when we have gone. And even when you go you will look after him from heaven. This is our faith. Death can never separate us from those we love.

❦ **FATHER**, lover of life, you never take back any of your gifts which you give me. Life is your gift to me so that even in death I do not lose my life but change it for something more perfect. In my new life I shall see you face to face, and know you in a way that is impossible as long as I remain in my mortal body. Teach me then to value my life now, so that I live each day to the full. Life comes to me moment by moment. Encourage me not to waste a single moment by worrying about the future, especially about what will happen to my loved ones when you come to call me home to you. May I trust them and myself to your tender loving care in which we find our inner peace which nothing can disturb.

My New Year resolutions

I always make and break my New Year resolutions. This affects every aspect of my life – physical, emotional and spiritual. Why does this happen? I feel I'm no good.

DAVID

You are good. At least you keep on trying. You make your resolutions even though going only on results achieved you should have given up years ago. St Paul would sympathise with you. He saw himself at times as a 'wretched man' (Romans 8:24). 'Instead of doing the good things I want to do', he wrote, 'I find myself doing the things I do not want' (Romans 8:9).

We all aim higher than we are able to reach and this is

good. As Christians we want to be perfect. But who is? We keep on trying despite our failings. The big thing is that we pick ourselves up every time we fall. We may not win many battles but we have a right and duty to claim the victory. With God on our side nothing good is beyond our reach, no failure can put us down permanently.

So, David, keep wanting to change into a better person, while at the same time realising that you have a long way to go yet. Take one step at a time. Be glad you have made it but don't stop and stay there. We are pilgrims. I want to see healing services as a regular feature in every parish in this country next year. It may not happen, but I'm going to have a good try. This is my New Year resolution. Will you make it yours for your parish?

❦ LORD, you know me better than I know myself. I am forever making resolutions which I never seem able to fulfil. Despite my failings over the years, I have never given up hoping that tomorrow will be a better day. Put in my heart the determination I need to continue making resolutions and the courage to see them through so that one day they will become a reality.

I am terrified of hell

I am literally terrified of hell. I try not to be, but it is always there at the back of my mind. I obey all the Church's rules, but I still feel that I will never get to heaven. How can I get rid of my fears?

KATHLEEN

Fear is one of the most destructive forces which we have to learn to control. As a Catholic you should be thinking of heaven, not hell. If you read the Gospels you will see that Christ came to heal us and prepare us for sharing his home

13

with God his Father. He said that in his Father's house there were many mansions. Heaven is your destiny and mine. Christ will not fail us and we must not allow ourselves to think that we will fail him. You are not going to lose out if you do your best. That is good enough for God. You will only be perfect in the next world, not in this.

Of course you are not certain that you are saved, Kathleen. Nobody is. The other day a Pentecostalist asked me if I wanted to be 'saved'. I said that of course I did. He went on to explain how I could be certain I would be 'saved'. He was quite wrong and I told him so. No one is certain that they are saved. We can only *hope* we are. Our hope is in Christ and we could have no better reason.

Kathleen, put your fears aside. You and I and millions like us are *on our way* to heaven as pilgrims. And we will make it together. Forget your horror movie in your mind. Switch channels from hell to heaven. Then you will have got the Gospel message in focus. Your vision of life in this world as well as the next will improve.

❧ JESUS, our life and peace, grant me the grace to believe in your love and mercy. Because you love and understand me, you are merciful in forgiving me all my wrongdoing and weakness. You know that I live in a world damaged by sin, and I need to be protected even from myself. You are my shepherd and guide, and with you by my side I have nothing to fear. My love for you casts out my fear. Teach me to concentrate on your goodness rather than my failings. May I grow in an assurance that when my life on this earth draws to an end, you will bring me home to your Father to live in love and peace.

Christmas peace in Belfast

In 1994, we were blessed in Belfast with our first wonderful, peaceful Christmas in twenty-five years. Our hopes of peace are again slowly diminishing. Will you please pray for peace for our people, Catholic and Protestant?

MARTIN

Of course I will. I have prayed for peace in Northern Ireland ever since the violence really erupted in 1968. For three years I worked for peace in the North where I experienced for myself the anguish, fear, frustration and hopelessness of the people on both sides of the religious divide. The cause of the problem was not one-sided. I often felt as I marched, campaigned, and prayed for peace that we in the Church were also very much part of the problem and the division. We cannot wash our hands of all the blame.

I saw the physical barrier of the peace line in Belfast as an external sign of something much deeper in people's minds, hearts and attitudes. I knew their yearnings for peace, and the tears that were wept for their loved ones so cruelly and unnecessarily taken from them. I perhaps was as excited as you in 1994 as you celebrated your first peaceful Christmas in over twenty-five years. I now share your anxiety that the clouds of violence may see a return to the bad old days.

We all need to pray for peace for you and your people, whether Catholic or Protestant. Only God can change people's hearts. I pray for that. Especially for a true conversion of your leaders. We look forward in hope. Peace be with you.

❦ **FATHER**, you sent your angels to sing of peace on earth to all those of goodwill. May the Spirit of Christ come again into the minds and hearts of all those in violent situations. May those who are at peace with one another hold fast to the goodwill that unites them, and may those who are enemies forget their hatred and listen to the message of peace. Help me today to be at peace in my mind and heart so that through your power it may spread to all those whom I encounter. May no word or action of mine disturb their peace or mine.

Insanely jealous

I am insanely jealous of other people's success. I hate myself for it, but I cannot seem to be able to change. Why is this happening to me?

JANE

Like an alcoholic, the first step to your healing is to acknowledge that you are jealous. Now, with God's help, you can begin to do something about it. You realise how destructive it is, not only of yourself, but of your relationship with other people. A jealous person is insecure. He wants what other people have which he hasn't got. It is a form of greed. Jealousy can stretch its destructive vapour into every aspect of life, so you are unable to breathe properly. Jealousy suffocates you. Jane, recognise it for what it is and treat it as you would treat cancer. As soon as jealousy rears its ugly head, see it as your enemy. Question it. Ask yourself, why am I jealous of this person? Am I being fair in my assessment and attitude to him? Am I allowing jealousy to take me into negative thoughts and actions so that it dominates my life? Am I destroying my own inner peace and happiness by my jealousy?

Let people be of whom you are jealous, or who are jealous of you. Jealousy brings its own punishment. Love yourself in the sense that you are grateful for the gifts God has given you. Never mind about other people. If you are glad you are you, then why bother about what other people have or do.

☙ LORD JESUS, you were the victim of jealousy all through your humble life. The leaders of your own people felt

16

threatened by your mission of love and healing. They were afraid of losing their power as thousands flocked to you, even out into the desert. Secure in your Father's love, you loved people because this is what your Father wanted you to do. Teach me to be at peace within myself so that I never lose the awareness of God my Father's love for me. With this I am rich enough, and do not ask for anything more. May I learn to be glad at other people's happiness and fulfilment so that I see it as a blessing for them rather than as a threat to me.

Now for the Good News

Christmas without people with whom we love and share our lives is meaningless. Every Christmas in my forty-five years as a priest has been different. I remember my very first Christmas which is as clear to me now as if it happened only yesterday.

It was Christmas Eve morning and we were putting the final touches to the crib. There was the usual bustle and excitement as the parishioners lovingly got everything ready for Midnight Mass. I was as excited as they were. Mary and her husband were there. They were really loving and dedicated Catholics and my close friends.

In conversation I asked them if everything was ready in their own home, all the cards sent, the presents bought. Mary told me that there was one person to whom she had not sent a Christmas card. It was her brother, Brendan. He had married in a registry office ten years before and given up the practice of his religion. The family had cut him off. I saw Mary was hurting inside, and as her brother lived fairly near, I advised her to go and see him. It was too late to send him a Christmas card.

Later that afternoon she was back ringing at my front door. Apparently Brendan was in the last stages of cancer and she asked me to come and pray with him. I went with her immediately and for over an hour I shared with Brendan his worries

17

and fears and his sadness at the hurt he had caused his parents. He made his peace with God and received the sacraments, including confession and the blessing of his marriage. I saw that Mary and her husband were in tears. Brendan died on Christmas Day. I shall always remember him. Christmas is a time for peace and reconciliation.

FR MICHAEL

❦ **ALMIGHTY FATHER**, be with all those who grieve today over the loss of a loved one. May their sorrow be lit up with the brightness of the resurrection so that they may be assured that they will meet again those whom they have loved and lost awhile. May they know that they are never parted from each other if they are united in Jesus your Son. He said, 'Blessed are those who mourn, they shall be comforted.' May he comfort those who grieve today, and strengthen their belief in life after death.

What does deliverance mean?

I have been to a healer who tells me that I have an evil spirit in me and need deliverance. I am frightened and have nightmares about being in the power of Satan and that eventually I shall go to hell. How can I be freed from that?

JENNIE

One of the largest growing numbers today in any 'profession' is to be found among those non-Christians who call themselves 'healers'. Many of these dabble in the occult and you, Jennie, are one of their patients or victims. All over the country, cities such as Birmingham, Glasgow and London hold 'Spiritual Mind and Body Festivals' which draw thousands of people. I have encountered many disorientated people who have dabbled with ouija boards, consulted clairvoyants and tarot card readers. Genuine psychiatrists are

18

extremely worried about the disastrous results which follow this addiction and some fear that by the next decade one in ten of the population in this country will have serious problems arising from the practice of the occult. I have no reason to doubt that figure.

There is also a preoccupation with Satan. He is seen as the only cause of all illness whether it be emotional, physical or spiritual. So deliverance is the order of the day. The reasoning goes that because Jesus delivered people from demons so should we. There is great need for prayer and discernment before we start deliverance. It is a very special ministry and I know priests who have special gifts for this type of healing.

So Jennie, I suggest you go to a prayerful priest who knows his God and his people. He will help you through the trauma of what you are going through. The nightmares will end and the dawn of inner peace which is Christ's gift to you will brighten up your life. God wants you whole, healthy and happy. Concentrate on the love Jesus has for you. He has already won the battle with Satan. Claim the victory and you will find peace.

❦ JESUS, you have won the victory over Satan. I should be thinking of you and your triumph rather than concentrating on the power of Satan. I praise you for the example of the people whose belief in your resurrection has brought me deep inner peace which nothing or no one can destroy. I am conscious that Satan would like me to think that he has power over me, but my faith in your victory overcomes all his attempts to trap me into thinking of him rather than of you. I pray for all those caught in this snare so that they may be delivered and become free to acknowledge you as Lord and Saviour of their lives in whom there is perfect peace and happiness.

I'm afraid of change

I am afraid of change, especially in religion. I want things to stay as they are. Why is the Church changing so much? I don't feel secure in it any more. Am I wrong to resist change?

BRIAN

Life means change. We change every day because life is a growing, changing process. I understand exactly how you feel. The things in the Church that meant so much to you in years gone by are no longer there. You miss them, and wish they were back again. You are suffering from nostalgia and Christians cannot afford the luxury of nostalgia. You cannot put the clock back. We live in today's not yesterday's world.

You are right. Religion gives security. Faith *challenges* us. It presents us with the problems of today, and how we can face up to them in a Christian way. Look at the history of the Church from the Council of Jerusalem in the first century right up to recent times.

Read Acts 11 and 15. James, Peter and Paul had to come to terms with allowing Gentiles into their community. If they had not accepted change, then there would be no Christian Church and we would still be Gentiles. They were guided by the Spirit. We need the Spirit's guidance, too, so that we grow as Christian persons in our changing Church and world. Religion without faith is like a ship turned into a houseboat. We live in it and it makes us feel safe tied to its moorings whereas it was meant to sail the seas.

Cheer up, Brian. On my desk is a little card which says 'Change is here to stay'. The only permanent thing in our world is change. You have to learn to live with it in faith.

❦ **LORD JESUS**, each one of us needs your vision and courage if we are to grow as fulfilled people in a changing world. You changed the world of your followers when you preached and lived out your Gospel of how your Father meant us to live if we were to seek his kingdom. You came to a kingdom where people had lost the dream which was part of their heritage left to them years before by their leaders. Come again, Jesus, into my life, and fill me with your Spirit so that I may renew the dream you have for me. Rekindle the fire of my enthusiasm for the challenge of your message so that it changes me and those whom I meet. We need to recapture the spirit of the Early Church so that the world will know that you are alive. Send a wonderful outpouring on us all so that in all the changes which happen, we see your Spirit at work, bringing us hope for the future and making our dreams come true.

The agony of divorce

I suffer from panic attacks and agoraphobia brought on by stress from a broken marriage and a long legal battle over the custody of my two children. After 27 years of marriage I am sorry to say I was a battered wife, but one who never told anyone. I face a legal bill the size of a mortgage. I feel I cannot cope any more. What am I to do?

VERONICA

The breakup of marriage is very painful. The after-effects are even worse. It is obvious that you could not have remained under the same roof with a husband who used physical violence. It is all very well to say 'you have made your own bed and you must lie in it'. I do not agree with that where your peace of mind is at stake. I have always confronted husbands who are violent in the home. I have been told it is not my business. Of course, I know it is. What a shame you were not able to share your physical and mental suffering with someone who understood you. As a result you have been bruised in your spirit, and need help in order to regain your peace of mind and heart. This will take time, Veronica, so be patient with yourself. I pray for you and the thousands like you who have to go through the shredding process of a bitter

21

divorce. You need inner peace which only God can give you. I pray for this gift for you.

✝ JESUS, lover of the family, I pray for your blessing on all those who suffer the pain of rejection in their married life. Many feel so deserted by their spouse with whom they have shared much of their lives that now they feel less of a person. They have many hurtful memories which they are unable to share with anyone so that the secrets lie buried within them. May they never fester and grow into a bitterness which destroys them, and brings their lives to a standstill. As they pick up the pieces of their lives again, be with them, Lord, and lead them gently into a life which will restore their self-value and give them the courage to face the future with calmness, hope and peace. Heal them, Lord, as only you know how.

The fear of loneliness

I am lonely. I just cannot make friends however hard I try. What's wrong with me? How do you go about making friends?

KAREN

If you have no friends then you are really lonely. Jesus needed friends. This is what he called his apostles: 'I call you friends' (John 15:15). We were not meant to live on a lonely island without companions. We are part of the human family, and in God's eyes we are each other's brothers and sisters. You will never know yourself, Karen, until you move outside your own island, and be prepared to share yourself with others. We are in ourselves what friends make us.

So how do you 'make' friends? It is not all that easy. We will be tempted to call acquaintances 'friends' but this is a short and treacherous path to follow. There are no short cuts to friendship. We meet and discover friends in moments of great joy or sorrow. So it was with Jesus. He shared the triumph of his

22

transfiguration and his agony in the garden of Gethsemane with his special friends, Peter, James and John. It is in these special moments in our lives that we come closest to each other.

Wait for that moment, Karen. Be patient with yourself. When the time is right you will know true friendship for what it is. It will be well worth the waiting. You cannot make friends. They will just happen. In them you will come alive and discover yourself.

❦ FATHER, you did not mean us to live alone, or to live for ourselves alone. You set us down in a family context where we would be nurtured and grow to our fullness as persons. In my gratitude to you for giving me my family and friends, who are very much part of me, I pray for all those who are lonely, and feel that no one cares about them. Loneliness can be a very destructive force which clouds over the brightest day and chills the heart of those who suffer its hidden pain. Fill the hearts and minds, of lonely people Father, with sweet memories of those in the past who were kind to them. Send them friends to warm their lives and heal the pain of past memories of loneliness and rejection.

How can my wife share my faith?

My wife is a good gentle person whom I love dearly. We share everything together except my Catholic faith. I miss the fact that she is not part of something which is so precious to me. I'm afraid of forcing my beliefs on her while at the same time I would love to encourage her to become a Catholic. What is the best way forward?

TED

You are very blessed to have such a loving wife. She is God's gift to you. You share in so much already and my advice is to concentrate on that. If faith is a gift from God for which we

23

can pray, but never deserve, in her own way I'm sure your wife loves God even though perhaps not in a religious setting. Why? I just don't know. Quietly, without making a show of it, pray for God to give her the special gift which you have.

There is of course a big distinction between religion and faith. Faith as I said is God's gift; religion is how we express it in human terms. There are many people with faith who do not attend church, just as there are some people who go to church regularly but who are lacking in faith. Be a good, loving Christian and in a way which you perhaps will not understand you are preparing your wife for God's gift when it comes. Be patient. No force feeding! In the special moments of joy and sorrow in your lives there will be opportunities for you to share your faith together. In the meantime be thankful for the good things with which the Lord has blessed you both.

☙ **HOLY SPIRIT**, I give you thanks that you have blessed me with the gift of faith. It is a precious gift which I want to share with others, especially with those whom I love so that we can come closer together. Jesus wants us to spread his good news of love, hope and peace to a world which has not yet learned to believe in him. Give to my life a deepening awareness of my faith, and a growing sensitivity to the needs of others, so that through my lifestyle, I may prepare them to receive the gift of Christian faith. Be with husbands and wives today who yearn that their partners may share their faith, and grant that their prayers be answered.

Worry and asthma

My youngest child, Jennie, has asthma and I worry a lot about her. Her condition seems to be getting worse. Can her condition be healed?

SARAH

24

You worry about Jennie because you want what is best for her. It hurts you to see her suffer. The most important thing for her at the moment is to know that *you are at peace within yourself* and that her condition is not causing you distress. In this way you are healing her. Let me tell you a story.

Five years ago I was called to a hospital in Ireland where a young girl of 14 was in intensive care because of extremely advanced asthma. I checked her story out. Her mother had died seven years previously and she idolised her father. She wanted to protect him in every situation. He had a heart condition and was in the same hospital undergoing a bypass operation. I saw him first. He was making a wonderful recovery after the operation and his prognosis was excellent. I reassured his daughter about him, and I could see that immediately her breathing improved. I saw both father and daughter the following week, not in hospital, but in their home.

So if you leave your daughter's condition in God's hands and stop worrying, you will find inner peace. This is the best healing medicine you can give your daughter. Jennie will know you are at peace because she is probably very sensitive to you, and she in turn will stop worrying. Asthma is very much an emotional as well as a physical condition. You and your daughter will heal each other as together you discover God's peace for you both. Peace be with and within you.

❦ **SPIRIT OF GOD**, whose breath fills us with life, breathe today on all those who suffer from asthma. You alone can heal them and bring them peace. Ease the worry of those who are close to them, especially their parents. Help them to realise that anxiety is often transmitted from one to the other. May they realise the value of taking life placidly as your Spirit moves gently into their lives and brings them inner peace.

When you lose confidence

I have no confidence in myself mainly because my father always ran me down on every possible occasion. I am unable to cope in business or in personal relationships because I feel so inadequate. I hate my father for what he has done to me.

BRIAN

Your father should have loved you as his son and been proud of you. It was his duty and privilege to encourage you to grow up and be the kind of person who would be content with life and be happy with yourself. He failed you miserably, I'm afraid, and you are right in diagnosing your own lack of self love.

What was your own father's background? Was it the same as yours? Is it a case of the sins of the parents being visited on the children? If so, then he is to be pitied as well as blamed. He has missed out on so much that is beautiful in the growing relationship between a father and his son. Parents pass on not only their own physical characteristics but their emotions and attitudes as well. Don't hate your father. Forgive him and feel sorry for him.

As for yourself, my advice is to accept that you have been damaged. Concentrate on the good aspects of your personality and develop them. Find a friend or friends with whom you can share and who will help you to grow in confidence and self-esteem. It may well be a slow process, but the end result will be well worth the effort. Your father made you feel like a budgie when you were really an eagle. Don't be confined by your little cage. Fly out of it to a new, freer, brighter future. Leave the nest of the past and be yourself.

❦ **FATHER**, we all need confidence if we are to love ourselves, and achieve the purpose for which you made us. We are all damaged in varying degrees due to different circumstances. We need self-assurance if we are to make our way in the world. I praise you for those in my life who encouraged me to see something of value in myself which enabled me to face life with calmness and confidence. Help those who have been damaged in their family and have never fully recovered. Let your Spirit come into their minds and hearts so that they will appreciate why their parents, or those closely associated with them, behaved the way they did. As your children, may they live in the present, confident that living life now is the best way to heal the unhappy memories of the past.

Now for the Good News

I am a priest who has been converted to inner healing because of what happened in my parish. My people were extremely keen for me to have an El Shaddai healing service and I asked you to come, not because I believed in healing, but rather to be open to my people. I did not concelebrate with you because I was not sure what was going to happen, so I prayed and observed from the back of the church.

Everyone seemed happy, relaxed and prayerful in the packed church. It was quite impressive and I felt God was there. You spoke about forgiveness and how important it was in our Christian lives. You said we were to pray for each other to be given the grace to forgive someone who hurt us the most.

My eyes fixed on Bridget, one of my best parishioners. She was very bitter with Jim, another parishioner who was once a close friend of the family, but who, under the guise of friendship, had sexually abused her teenage daughter. The hatred in her heart was destroying her life. For months I had tried to help her, but to no avail.

A miracle was needed. I saw Jim at the other side of the church. I knew that he was heartbroken by what he had done. If ever a man was sorry he was, but the barrier between them was too great for any human attempt at reconciliation. I said to God, 'Please let Bridget forgive him at this service today and I will believe in healing.' I prayed for them both as never before. It was that kind of service. Then, at the sign of peace, it hap-

pened. Bridget got up from her pew and went over to Jim and obviously spoke words of forgiveness to him. He broke down and cried. As for me, well I was on the verge of tears too, but I did not want anyone to see me crying so I slipped out into the courtyard. The next time you came to our parish I concelebrated with you. I believed in healing!

FR BILL

❦ **FATHER**, may I grow in my belief in the power of your Son, Jesus Christ, to continue his work of healing in his Church. I pray for priests who have never been taught the beauty of the ministry of healing in their preparation for the priesthood. May people who have experienced healing in their own lives encourage their priests to foster healing services in their parishes. May they be open to the workings of the Holy Spirit who will show them ways of how people are healed. May priests realise that healing is so essential to the Christian message that without it there is no Gospel to preach.

When we meet again in heaven

My Dad died recently just a week after being released from hospital. I always found it difficult to talk to him, probably because when we were kids he was rather frightening. I wanted to get on with him but I never did. Will I be able to put things right in the next world when I meet him again? I feel so guilty about our relationship.

DAMIAN

You never grew up in your relationship with your Dad. You were never really friends. It was the wrong father-child attitude which is very destructive of personal growth. Parents have to allow their children to become adults. The only one who *remains* the Father of us all is God himself.

In heaven we will be brothers and sisters and there will be

a whole new relationship between parents and their children. You and your Dad will see each other in a wonderfully loving relationship where all the pain and wrong attitudes of the past are forgotten. Now Damian, that is something to look forward to so don't worry about the past. In heaven your Dad and you will be changed. It will be a whole new world of never-ending friendship.

❦ FATHER, your Son Jesus told us that in your house there are many mansions. This belief in you and your generosity helps me to believe in life after death. I look forward to meeting my parents, brothers, sisters, friends and all those with whom I shared my life on earth in your time because there is room for us all. My belief in the resurrection is my anchor of hope which keeps the frail boat of my faith secure in the face of storms and tempest.

My grief is mellowed by the knowledge that death is only a parting for a little while from those whom we love and who love us. May we see our friends and family as a great cloud witnesses from heaven, surrounding us on all sides on earth encouraging us to believe that where they are now we will be one day to share with them in their joy and happiness.

Is there forgiveness for abortion?

I am the father of a very committed Catholic family. One of my daughters became pregnant while studying for her 'A' levels. She and my wife put pressure on me to allow her to have an abortion. I did this reluctantly because I have always adhered strictly to the rules of the Catholic Church. Now my conscience will not let me rest. Will I be forgiven? Can I take Communion? The priest in confession tells me I am forgiven, but I can't forgive myself.

EDWARD

You must forgive yourself. Have sympathy and compassion for your wife and daughter. What is done is done and cannot be undone. The unborn child is in God the Father's loving care, and nothing could be better than that. It was wrong to take a human life and your family, especially your daughter, has to learn to live and to cope with that. There were all sorts of pressures at work in a very emotional situation. At that time it was hard to see beyond the present moment. In our inner healing movement we have to deal with the after-effects of abortion in the emotional and spiritual lives of the mother. They often wonder if they will be forgiven. This happens, too, with non-believers who have to keep the secret to themselves.

You have to find inner peace for yourself and help your family to find it. You say your conscience won't let you forgive yourself. It needs faith to affirm our belief in a forgiving God and I pray that your faith will grow stronger. Your faith enables you to believe in sin and makes you feel guilt about it. Your faith should also teach you to believe in a forgiving God. You cannot let the past destroy the quality of your life. So when the priest tells you that your sins are forgiven you must trust him. Jesus told the woman taken in adultery 'go your way and sin no more' (John 8:11).

You need the healing sacrament of Communion where you meet Christ the healer. He will soothe your guilt and the pain of your conscience. You will have more cause to thank him because he does not condemn you, and wants you from now on to live in peace. Feeling guilty will not bring the baby back. You have to live in the present. Live in peace with yourself and your wife and your daughter and God who is the loving Father of you all, including your unborn grandchild.

❦ HOLY SPIRIT of love and forgiveness, you teach us that there is no such thing as an unforgiveable sin for which we feel true sorrow. I thank you that you have taken my guilt of the past away, and lifted me up so that I could begin my life anew. Be with all those who feel weighed down by their past misdeeds, and cannot find any true lasting peace in their lives. Their sins are ever before them so that the past destroys the quality of their present lives. Only you, Holy Spirit, can lift them up and heal their memories. In learning from the past, may they give you thanks for your love and mercy as they live the rest of their lives in peace, free from fear and guilt.

Now for the Good News

I would like to answer the lady called Madge who wrote to you in the Universe *last week. She asked why God gives us so much pain.*

Almighty God does from time to time test our faith or trust in him. He never inflicts suffering on us, but will allow suffering to continue, in order to strengthen our faith (trust) in him. God is not a dual spirit, pain or love. He is only pure goodness, pure love. Madge has a golden opportunity to offer to him, the one gift he hasn't given her – suffering.

More than twelve years ago now I, too, experienced my father-in-law terminally ill for nine months before he died, followed by my Dad's death within months; my husband in a terrible state of shock, my son taken into hospital the day before the funeral with suspected meningitis. Needless to say, coping with all this in such a short time, I had a nervous breakdown. During my darkest days, which were many, I came to realise that Jesus was with me at the bottom of the deep pit that I found myself in. He pulled me up, out of that pit not overnight, but day by day a little at a time. Together with him I climbed back into life, not an easy life, to face more sickness in my family.

I must quote Padre Pio. Too much sorrow creates a desert. Truly my heart goes out to Madge and her family. I pray that she will soon have a little peace in her life. I urge her to stay

31

with her prayers. They do get answered often in the strangest ways. She can stop talking to God, but he will never forget her.

I write this in gratitude for the many blessings I have received in my life.

WENDY

❦ **HEAVENLY FATHER**, I thank you that all through my life you have watched over me with a father's love and never caused me a needless tear. There were times when unexpected calamities came my way, and I sought you but you seemed to hide your face from me. I felt alone, and yet you were there all the time watching over me, although I was too full of my own pain to be aware of your presence. You are now so much part of me that I believe that no matter what happens to me in the future, I shall never be afraid. When I walked in the valley of darkness, you were there with your crook and staff to give me comfort. Be with all those today who suffer distress so that they cannot see the way ahead. Take them by the hand and gently lead them out to pastures new where they will find hope and peace.

Searching for my daughter

In 1946 I had a daughter. I was not married. I loved my daughter and kept her with me for two years. Then I met my future husband and I decided to have my little girl adopted. My husband died 32 years ago and I am blessed with five wonderful children whom I love dearly but I have never forgotten my little girl who would now be 50. Should I search for her or leave things alone? I am 73 years old and this has been on my mind for a life time.

JUDY

You have to decide for yourself. I cannot do it for you. My first reaction is to let things be. Count your blessings. You

32

were blessed with a loving husband and now your children are your comfort. Why worry yourself about your daughter? Let her be. Think of the effect it might have on her. Will it be for her happiness and that of your five other children? How would they react? What good will it do anyone in the final analysis? You love all *six* of them.

You have done your best. It is too late now to go back over the past ground which has not been visited for all these years. Be at peace yourself, Judy.

Pray for all your children. God is looking after each one of you. You are *all* part of the same family. He does not love anyone more or less than the other. You feel the same towards all your children. Keep your first-born in your heart. In love you will meet again.

Let nothing disturb you. Leave your daughter in God's hands. She is a grown woman, probably with her own family. You wish her well and want everything that is best for her. You must not feel guilty about what happened in the past. You did what you thought was best at the time. If you have any misgivings then let the person you are today heal the person you were when you decided to have your daughter adopted.

❦ **LORD JESUS**, your mother Mary came seeking you for three days when she lost you in Jerusalem. You caused her anxiety as she wondered where you were. Even though you said you were about your father's business, nevertheless it is strange that one so sensitive and caring as you caused so much anguish to Mary and Joseph. I pray for all parents who search for their children because they are part of them, and want to know how they are faring in their lives. Many parents grieve at the loss of children who no longer make contact and cause them undue anxiety and pain. Jesus, I pray that parents trust their children to your tender care, and, good shepherd that you are, may you bring back to the fold of the family the lambs that were lost.

33

How do I know a genuine healer?

I've been to a prayer group where some members always want to lay hands on me, but I never see them asking for healing for themselves. I'm not happy about that. What do you think?

MONICA

You ring alarm bells in my memory. From my own experience those who claim to minister healing but never ask for someone to pray for themselves are *rarely genuine*. They seem to want to stand on higher ground, as if they themselves are so perfect that they don't need healing. We all do. That is why I always ask the congregation to whom I minister to pray for me first.

Once we start to claim healing in our own name and power then we have put ourselves outside the boundaries of the ministry of Christ, the humble suffering servant. We are only servants of Christ's power, and unless we suffer we will never be true ministers of this special healing gift. It is a demanding ministry which challenges our faith. I have far too often met people who claim divine power within themselves who are an easy prey for the devil. Ministers of healing are *ordinary* people. Jesus alone is *extraordinary* in that he humbly works through those he has gifted with his ministry.

Healing is an ideal platform from which to launch an ego trip. I have seen the counterfeit fall, and yet people in extreme need of healing go to them with disastrous effects. If I were you, Monica, I would never allow anyone to pray over me or lay hands on me unless and until you are convinced that they are genuine. We have our fair share of Walter Mitty's in the healing ministry. They are only a 'hired man who has no concern for the sheep' (John 10:13). Simple people who are hurting inside are easy targets for unchristian attitudes which look on healing in terms of power rather than service. They hinder the true Christian Gospel.

❦ **JESUS**, you alone are our wounded healer. I believe in you

34

because in all your works you did the will of your Father, and never sought your own glory. You are the genuine healer who exercised your ministry so that those who witnessed it would give glory to God the Father. You were Father-orientated and your life was one of prayer. You healed people because you loved them, and never worked miracles in order to be popular. Your humility in acknowledging the source of your power drew people to give thanks to God the Father. Lord Jesus, our healer, teach us that when we pray for healing for others in your name, we may act and think as you did so that people will see you at work and prayer in our ministry. May they believe that you are alive and healing people in today's world.

I want my mum to be healed

My Mum is the best person I know. The doctors say she is dying of cancer but I'm not ready to accept that. I want her to get better again. If she dies I just don't know how I shall cope. Am I wrong to keep on praying for her healing?

SUE

How right you are to want your mother to live. Aren't you blessed to have her? Look at the influence she has had on your life. She has obviously shown you the value of your faith. That is why you keep on praying for her healing against all the odds, and why shouldn't you?

Of course you must keep on praying. It may require a miracle to heal your mother but we pray to the God of the living not the dead. Your prayer is the source of your hope. You pray not only because you love your mother but because you believe in a God who listens to your prayers. Don't give up, Sue.

And the future? Don't worry about tomorrow. God will look after you then just as he did through your mother all through your life. Tomorrow is the enemy of today.

Tomorrow will look after itself. Together today we pray for your mother's health. We live in hope. Do not let anyone dampen your hope. They are pessimists and fatalists who are afraid to hope. Sue, keep on praying and hoping. God is our Father with whom nothing is impossible.

❦ JESUS, healer of the sick, who raised the dead to life, I praise you for the faith you gave me to keep on hoping and praying for those who are ill. You know what is best for each one for whom I pray, so I leave the final outcome to your tender mercy. Listen, I beseech you, to the silent tears of those who weep inside their spirits as they yearn to see their loved ones made whole and well again. Your healing of people was the centre of your earthly message so that where healing is absent then there is no gospel to be preached, or witness we can give that you are alive and heal today. In the face of the most severe medical and psychological diagnosis, may we continue to pray for those who are seriously ill, and may your inner peace come to us all, which is ultimate healing.

I wanted to marry

All my life I have longed to get married and have a family. It has not worked out that way. I am now in my late forties and I dread the future of living alone. With the break up of so many marriages, why didn't God send me someone with whom I could share my life?

SARAH

I feel sorry for you. You raise many questions which I am often asked and for which there is no easy answer. What way do you live your life? Apart from this very great void, do you give your time to the service of others? There must be a reason why you have not found the 'right person', but it is hidden from your eyes at the moment. Our faith tells us there is a

36

purpose for everything so I shall pray that you have a clearer understanding of why your wishes have not been realised.

Pray, too, for people in marriage that they realise how sharing in friendship is essential to any true marriage relationship. Leave the future, Sarah, to God. That is not a platitude. It is the best, and sometimes the only, thing we can do.

❦ **FATHER**, you created man and woman, and gave them the ability and desire to multiply and fill the earth. There are many who feel rejected or abandoned by you because they have not met the right person with whom they feel they can share their lives. As their friends marry and form new relationships within the marriage context, they feel an increasing sense of being left out. Father, I thank you for my friends who so fill my life that I rarely, if ever, feel lonely. They brought me much of what is good in my life through the warmth of their friendship. They helped me to reach out to others and to you without fear of what it would cost me in the process. In thanking them I pray for those for whom each day is lonely. In their hearts their wish to share is not fulfilled. Grant that, if it be that they never find a partner, their lives will be filled with caring friends as a gift from you to brighten and fulfil their lives.

I grieve for the past

Years ago before I became a truly committed Christian I hurt someone very deeply. I do not know where she is and agonise over what I may have done to her. It affects my peace. What do you think I should do?

JAMES

We have to leave the past as well as the future to God. The only way for us to live is in the present. We feel *guilty* about the past and we are *fearful* of the future. Guilt and fear handcuff us so that we cannot live out our lives in the present one day at a time. Jesus knew how difficult life is and that is why he said that 'each day has enough troubles of its own' (Matthew 6:34). The one thing you must not do is worry about the past. Worry achieves nothing for anyone. So, James, let the past be. Commend the person you have hurt to the Lord's mercy.

You are suffering from *remorse*. You are unhappy in yourself for what has happened. You are a different person today from the person you were all those years ago. You acted differently then because you had a different set of values. Today you need to trust the Lord. Only he can put things right. You are sorry now. That is the main point. You have got to go on living believing that the Lord has forgiven you. The best restitution you can make is to resolve with God's grace never to hurt anyone like that again.

❦ **FATHER**, in our lifetime we may have hurt someone who has since passed out of our lives, and we have no way of contacting them. Free us from any guilt we have about the past which prevents us from living our Christian faith to the full as you would have us do. Liberate us from the kind of guilt which only helps to foster feelings of rejection of ourselves, and hides from us your all-embracing forgiveness. Only you can heal the wounds that have been made, and restore everyone to a proper understanding of what true sorrow really means. May all those who live in the shadow of the past walk out into the light of the present where there is freedom to grow as persons beloved of you.

And now for the Good News

I have been ill with cancer for over four years. At first I was both terrified and depressed. Every day I wondered what the future held in store for me. I was worried sick about leaving my husband, my children and my mother, who has not been well for a long time.

More in hope than expectation, I came to an El Shaddai healing service. Little did I realise that through it my whole life would change. I became a new person. I knew probably for the first time that God my Father loved me. He allowed me to have my illness so that he could truly enter my life with his love, and begin to heal not only me, but also my husband, my children and my mother. Every day since that service I have felt his presence in my whole life and my relationships. I still have physical problems, but now I know that he is touching all that I touch in my life with his healing love. All my relationships have become more loving and healing.

God is doing much more than I ever dreamed of asking him. I am at peace in my mind and heart and I am content to let him have his way and in his time. Thank you and your team of helpers for your special ministry. Even though I am many miles away from you, I still feel very much part of the family. Your books and tapes mean so much to me and to others to whom I lend them. I am not cured physically, but I am healed and I know now what it is to be truly alive. God's love for me changed my life. It is wonderful!

MARGARET

❦ **LORD JESUS**, when I am faced with difficult situations in my life which neither I nor anyone else can help me to solve, I turn to you as my last and only hope. You never fail me, even though at times the response seems a long time in coming. I thank you that you have answered my prayers for other people when those they loved were faced with the horrific consequences of a terminal disease. You raised them up, renewed their bodies, and gave them a new spirit of strength and light within them, conquering their weakness and darkness. I thank you Lord, for the power of your loving healing manifested in so many people who live today in our world because you answered their plea for health and for healing.

Stay with us all, Lord, so that we may remember that your age for healing is never past, and is with us today if only we learn to believe.

Married outside the Church

I read your healing article in the Universe *every week. I need a little help to heal me. I could do with your advice and prayers. My daughter has just got married. She got married in the Church of England and has not been going to Mass for nearly two years. She is a Christian girl and so is her husband. They have prayer groups which they take part in every week. They said they did not find enough community spirit within the Catholic Church which seems so sad. They both say they feel closer to God now, so it is me perhaps that needs the healing. It is just, Monsignor, that I feel her marriage is not right because it was not in the Catholic Church.*

JOAN

Joan, you have touched a raw nerve with many other Catholic parents. You are obviously a caring, loving mother which is shown by the way your daughter and her husband share so openly with you. I thank God they have experienced Christ in their lives to the extent that prayer is so important to them. You should praise them for that, because prayer can do nothing but good in their lives. It is unfortunate that they did not find the same loving community spirit in their own parish. This is not uncommon and like you it saddens me that they are lost to the Church but, thankfully, not to God. I have met many like them who have drifted away from our Church because they did not feel they belonged. You are right not to blame them, but don't blame yourself either. You have obviously done your best as a parent, but it is not enough. We do not support families and individuals enough so that they have an experience and realisation of how important the

Catholic Church is in their lives. The Church will only come alive for people when they see that we care about every aspect of their lives and not just about Church rules and regulations. Faith is all about loving God and this is the essential message of the Catholic Church and every organisation that dares to call itself Christian.

You say you need healing. Don't we all! Let your daughter see how much you too love God and her, and that you appreciate how important the Christian faith is for you both. As regards getting married in the Catholic Church, we will pray for that. It will come in God's good time. Don't worry about it. Your daughter knows how you feel about it. Her prayers will lead her to do the right thing. Be thankful that she sees God as the important person in her life. He is her Father and understands her far more than you, or I, or anyone else.

❦ JESUS, you taught us that the one commandment your followers must always follow is to love one another as you have loved them. I pray that all the rules and directions of Christian Churches may flow from this love you have for people as children of your Father. I thank you for those in the Church whose lives have mirrored this love and encouraged me to try to do the same. May no one feel excluded from this love, and may everyone know that God loves them as only a Father can. May I encourage them by my words and actions to believe in this healing truth, which lifts them up and gives them hope.

I want my husband to share my faith

I would love to share my faith with my husband, but he is just not interested. He says he is glad for me, that I get so much out of it, but that it is not his 'cup of tea'. What should I do?

HEATHER

I think I know how you feel. Marriage is a sharing; you share

41

so many things with your husband already, it is natural that you should want to be one with him in your prayer and worship. It is lonely going to Mass on your own, when it would be so much better if the one you loved was at your side.

But, Heather, you share your faith with him in a thousand and one hidden ways. He obviously appreciates this by the very fact that he acknowledges that you get so much out of your belief. He is happy for you because he loves you. Isn't that something? In other ways which he cannot express in words, he sees God at work in your life by what you say and do. You witness to God by your love for him.

Faith is a gift from God. You cannot teach the faith to someone, but you can lead them to it by your example and you are certainly doing that. Your husband is closer to the Christian faith than you think. When something special happens he will show his belief. Until that time comes, carry on as before. No pressure, no 'persuading', but just love him as someone whom God has given you to share your life.

❦ **LORD JESUS**, you shared your life and faith completely with your apostles. You were a family, and you called them your brothers and sisters. I thank you for my extended Christian family who have nurtured my belief, and shared in a way deeper than any human union. I remember with gratitude not only my parents and those united to me by blood, but also those whom I have met on my journey through life, the memory of whose faith warms my heart. Be with all those who yearn today to share their faith in you with those they love, and grant that their desires be fulfilled. May their love be enriched, and their cup of joy run over, as together in your loving family they praise your holy name.

No life of my own

My mother is very possessive. I look after her and she will not let me out of her sight. I have no life of my own. My future is bleak and lonely and I feel resentful that she has deprived me of what is my right. She is in her eighties and I am in my late fifties. Life has passed me by. I feel bitter. Please help me.

ANGELA

It is hard not to feel bitter and resentful. Your duty to your mother and yourself are in conflict. It is not easy to resolve the problem until all sides are examined. No one has the right to be so possessive of another that he or she is unable to live a full life as a mature person.

Parents should help us to grow and not keep us forever under their wings. We are, after all, eagles who were meant to fly, not budgies kept in a cage. At the same time, if you are the only one who has taken on the responsibility of looking after your mother, you are bound to feel guilty if you 'abandon' her now. Obviously this impossible situation in which you find yourself has been allowed to grow over the years. It seems too late to change now. You are in a great need of advice and help both physical and spiritual.

Angela, do not feel guilty about your angry feelings that you have been deprived of your rights. Others might not have felt so in a similar situation, but you do. It is quite natural to you. Accept the fact that you are bitter and it is destroying your inner peace. Now you can begin to do something about it in a positive way. You need to pray and find time when you can 'slip away' and feel free to be yourself. You have to be gentle but firm in doing this.

There is no easy answer: there never is in cases as complicated as yours. I need to know more about your situation and then perhaps I can give you clearer and more positive advice.

❦ LORD JESUS, you gave us the priorities we should have in our personal relationships. When you were told that your mother was anxious to have a word with you, you pointed to your disciples and said that they too were your family. Even though you loved your mother dearly, and she was at one with you, in your ministry you had to be yourself in order to fulfil your mission for which you came on earth. I thank you, Lord, that you showed me the need to be free in my human relationships so that I could be the kind of person you want me to be, and fulfil the mission to which you called me. I pray for all parents who find it difficult to give their children sufficient time and space in which to grow as persons in their own right. I remember also in prayer those who feel that they are being suffocated by a parental relationship. May they never become frustrated and bitter because they lack the courage to speak out in love to those who bind them so tightly to themselves, that they have little freedom of movement. I thank you for my own freedom, and for those who encouraged me to find it. Grant that by my life based on your example, I may help to inspire others to discover for themselves true Christian freedom.

Religious intolerance

My girlfriend is a Baptist and she is always criticising the Catholic Church. She is always on about 'Mary' and how idolatrous we are. I love her, but this antagonism to Catholics is becoming more prominent and dominates our conversation. What should I do?

BERNARD

If this criticism is 'done in the green wood then what will be done in the dry!' Far from decreasing, I think from my own experience that there is a real danger that it will become the rock on which your relationship will perish. It could well destroy your love for each other as it surfaces to challenge you. What does your faith mean to you? How do you see the future when you are married and your wife objects to your practising your religion? Will it affect the peace of your home? Will she agree to the Catholic upbringing of your children, or haven't you discussed this at all? Of course, you respect her faith, and her way of looking at religion, but if it is predominantly negative against the Catholic Church then you must be aware of the danger of unhappiness and heart-aches ahead.

Bernard, of course, we respect and understand the attitude of other Christian denominations. They are not all negative like your girlfriend. I have many caring Baptists who are very dear to me, but they do not threaten my religion, nor I theirs. My Catholic faith is very much part of my life. Without it I would feel lost. I suggest you both sit down and look at your relationship from every possible angle. See the difficulties ahead, evaluate them. Don't be starry-eyed. Stars don't shine in the cold light of day! I don't want to see either of you hurt. Faith and life are too precious for that. So I pray that the Spirit will show you what is the right thing to do. He will give you the courage to follow it through. The pain you both suffer now is better than allowing your differences to fester and grow.

❦ **HOLY SPIRIT**, we live in a global village called the world. Religion divides your people because the divisions are man-made. You breathe on us the gift of your Spirit which is faith which unites us together in one family. However, because of the cultural divisions which exist in various religions, we are different not so much in our hearts and aspirations, but in our customs and behaviour. I thank you, Holy Spirit, for the faith of all people everywhere who see a power beyond themselves as the source of their being and the preservation of their ongoing existence. I praise you for all Christians, whatever their religious affiliation, who believe in the lordship of Jesus Christ. I bless you for my faith, nourished in the Catholic Church which has given me so much that is of value in my life. I regret the divisions and prejudices which have done

45

much harm to the preaching and witness of the Christian Gospel. Only you, Holy Spirit, can make us one. We pray for this in the holy name of Jesus.

Now for the good news

I am writing to you with some very good news. Myself and my husband Brendan had been married nearly three years, and we both longed for a family. We had both been very ill during that time, my husband very seriously ill. The consultant had prepared us for very bad news. He thought my husband had cancer and was preparing to send him to hospital. Everybody was praying for us, and after my husband's operation the biopsy was normal to our great relief.

Then, last year I arranged a little weekend break for us in the North Yorkshire Moors, and then discovered through my mother's friends that you were going to be in Scarborough that very same weekend. It was the first time I had heard about you and your conferences on healing.

We attended on 28 May, and that afternoon you called us both up to you at the start of the healing session. You asked our names, and then asked us if we had a family, and would we like a family. Everybody, including the congregation prayed for us. We were very moved: my husband started to cry, and I felt very shaky. We left the conference feeling very uplifted with the whole experience.

And now to the good news. We are expecting a baby in July, just over a year later, and we are both overjoyed.

Since that day in Scarborough we have both said the El Shaddai prayer for healing, and I have also said the prayer for the unborn child. We are both very grateful for everybody's prayers on that special day. I knew you would want to share in our good news.

ANNE

❦ SPIRIT OF CREATION, the wonder of life finds its perfect
expression in the birth of a child. I thank you for the gift of
life, and that my mother and father considered each one
of my sisters and brothers as a blessing from you. I pray that
all parents will look on their children in such a way that they
never lose the wonder of how privileged they are to share
with you in creation. I thank you that in the ministry of
healing many husbands and wives were blessed with the gift
of a child and give you praise, glory and thanks for listening
to their plea.

I cannot say I'm sorry

*I just can't say I'm sorry even when I know I am wrong. My
father told me that to say you were sorry is a sign of weakness.
People say I am arrogant, but I'm not really. It is just psycho-
logically impossible for me to say the two words 'I'm sorry'.
Do I need healing?*

ANDREW

Your father was wrong and I'm not sorry for saying that! We
all make mistakes. It takes an honest person to admit they
are wrong. It involves courage. If you go through life never
admitting you are wrong *when you are*, then you are, in fact,
refusing to learn from your mistakes. You are not growing as
a person because you fail every time to jump the fence which
obliges you to say 'sorry'.

You are, or at least you seem to be, arrogant. Again, I'm
not sorry for that discernment. You presume you can afford
to carry on as if you had not been wrong. Isn't that arrogant?
Have you not a duty to say that *perhaps* you are not always
right? Do you really listen to the other person's point of
view? Are you aware that this attitude is destructive of
friendship?

I know you are not always wrong, but you are not always

47

right either. You need to take a good look at yourself. There is still time to change. If you don't then you are making the greatest mistake of your life. Jesus taught us the value of listening and being sensitive to other people's feelings and attitudes. If you think you made a mistake in writing to me, don't feel sorry about it this time. If you take what I say to heart then please God, when it is right for you to do so, you will be able to say and mean 'I'm sorry.'

❦ **LORD JESUS**, it is never easy for me to say that I am sorry, or to admit that I am wrong. Saying we are sorry is seen by many people as a sign of weakness and a giving in to the other person. You have taught me that while I must be prepared to stand up and be counted in the cause of truth, nevertheless, I should also be humble enough to acknowledge when I am wrong. Put your love of truth in my mind and heart so that I may always admit my mistakes and never be afraid to say that I am sorry. Bring peace and truth today to all those who are in conflict with each other. Teach us all to understand that to say we are sorry requires total honesty, courage and humility.

Will there be married people in heaven?

Jesus said that in heaven there will be no marrying or giving in marriage. Does that mean that the wife I loved and lost in death so tragically will no longer be my wife in the next world? I find that hard – in fact impossible – to accept. What did Jesus mean?
RICHARD

I am glad you raised the question which troubles so many people like you who have lost their beloved spouse and wonder what will be their relationship together in the next world.

Like everything else when Scripture is taken out of context, the wrong interpretation is given. When Jesus said there would be no marriage, he was replying to the Saddu-cees who did not believe in the resurrection (Mark 12:18–23). They posed to him the problem of a woman whose husband died leaving her childless. In turn she married the other six remaining brothers who died in turn leaving no children. So when they asked, 'Whose wife will she be?', they were really trying to catch Jesus out. They saw the resurrection as an extension of the present life. Marriage for them was solely for the procreation of children. They did not understand that after the resurrection there will be no need to procreate children, because marriage will take on a deeper spiritual meaning; their question was pointless. Jesus is saying that in heaven, marriage will change and the love of husband and wife will be deeper.

Richard, you will see your wife again. The happy relation-ship you shared together in marriage will bloom. Christ Jesus who worked his first miracle at the wedding feast of Cana shows us how beautiful married love is. It will never dis-appear. It will find its fulfilment in heaven. This is something to look forward to when you meet your beloved wife again.

❦ **LORD JESUS**, you witnessed to the beauty of human love at the wedding feast in Cana, and thereby gave us a better understanding of married love in this life and in the world to come. The power manifested in Christian marriage is that it is an expression of our love for you reflected in each other. Love never comes to an end. I have seen the loneliness and tears of those who have loved their spouses who died and wondered whether they would ever meet again. Their faith in you as their resurrection overcame their grief, finding consolation in your promise they no longer grieved as those who have no hope. In heaven, Lord, we shall love each other in a new and beautiful way so that the companionship we experienced in this life will grow to fulfilment. When we are with you and each other, there will be no more tears or parting, and love and life will be for ever.

Afraid to go to the doctor

I am afraid to go to my doctor in case he tells me I have cancer. I have awful pains in my stomach. Could it be cancer? I am afraid to find out. What should I do?

JENNIE

We all suffer from the cancer scare at some time in our lives. I know I did. Whenever I went to the doctor and he asked me was there anything else wrong with me, I always hurriedly said 'No'. I deliberately did not tell him of the pain I had in my stomach. When eventually I did pluck up enough courage to tell him, after a thorough medical examination he gave me a clean bill of health. Was I relieved!

Jennie, you are afraid. Fear is the great exaggerator which inhibits us and prevents us from trying to discover the truth. 'Inhibitor' is the name given to the devil. He really likes us to be afraid, even of God. So my advice to you is to go to your doctor, and tell him the truth. No matter what the result is, at least you will know what you have to face.

Say a prayer for guidance and inner peace. This fear you have of cancer is a sign of other fears in your life. When you have conquered this one, perhaps you will look quietly at other aspects of your life in which fear may be inhibiting you. The devil will not like it, but your guardian angel will be pleased.

❧ HOLY SPIRIT, teach us never to be afraid of finding out what is wrong with our body, mind or spirit. Ignorance is not bliss where my health is concerned. I need to seek the skill of those who have dedicated their lives to our medical and emotional care. I thank you for all doctors and nurses, and I pray that you will bless them as you give skill to their hands, discernment in their judgements and compassion in their hearts. Breathe into them your Spirit so that they may realise that they are not just dealing with a mind or a body, but with a whole person. May they see in all their patients the image of the wounded Christ.

Haunted by the past

I read your answers in the Universe *every week. I just cannot forget the past. Every time I prepare for confession I am frightened that I have kept some awful sin back in years gone by. Despite all my confessions I have not been to communion in years. I feel so unclean, so unworthy. Please help me.*

ALFIE

Those who told you that you were unclean and unworthy should be the ones going to confession. They have tied unsupportable burdens on your back. Jesus denounced the Pharisees for this very attitude (Matthew 23:4). He called them 'blind guides who strain at gnats and swallow camels' (Matthew 23:24). Read all of Chapter 23 of Matthew's gospel. It will help you understand how history is repeating itself today.

Now, Alfie, what can we do to help you? First of all, let us get back to basics. God loves you. If you don't accept that then there is not very much I can do for you. God understands you and knows when you are doing your best. He is not condemning you. You are condemning yourself. You are loveable because God made you so. The tragedy is that you have not been taught or encouraged to love yourself.

Unworthy? We are all unworthy. That is what makes God's love so wonderful. Accept it. If you cannot remember your sins then God gave you the loss of memory so that you would not haunt yourself with the past. Carry on living in the present.

❦ FATHER, in whom there is no past, only the present, teach me always to leave the past behind me, and to live in the

51

present moment, conscious of your loving presence and for-giveness. There have been times in the past, and will be in the future, when I needed to be healed of events which happened long ago, and which I now regret. At such times, fill me with an awareness of your mercy as my Father who forgives me especially when I find it difficult to forgive myself. All you ask of me is that I do my best now, and praise you for your forgiveness. Make me aware that the dawn of each new day is the beginning of my life, lived in the present and in your presence in which there is no past.

I am bored at Mass

I am a 'teenager' who finds Mass boring. I have told my parents and even though it hurt them, I had to be honest. I also told my parish priest, but he felt I should still come because it is my duty, even though I find Mass boring. I disagree. What do you think?

JERRY

It saddens me that so many young people like you do not find a response within the Church's worship. They say every Mass has the same value no matter who the priest is who says it and whether or not he tries to make it more relevant to young people like you. I disagree. If we ignore you young people, then our Church will be filled with just 'golden oldies'.

Years ago we had special Masses for youth. They are not so common nowadays. Why? Because our youth are integrated into our communities? Look around you this Sunday, Jerry, and you will see how few young people come to Mass any more. Are we acknowledging that we have lost them? I think we are discreetly silent about our lost young people. What a shame.

Jerry, I do not accept, and never could, this situation. If you leave then we are left with a geriatric congregation. We all need healing of set attitudes to churchmanship and worship. We have to change if we are to challenge young people. It is because I was challenged by a living parish when I was just twenty years of age that I decided to become a priest. I have still not lost the memory of it. I am still young at heart. Stay with us, Jerry, and together we will change things for the better.

✤ **JESUS CHRIST**, when you were on earth, people saw, heard and touched you as you walked and lived among them. Today, you live in your Church under sacramental signs so that we need faith to believe that you are still with us. It is impossible for anyone to convey your presence unless and until they experience you personally in their own lives. It is only when you showed yourself to me in people. Lord, that I became aware of your presence. I found you in the sick and the lonely; the young and the old, who were searching for a meaning to life; the rich and the poor who felt that there was something else more important than security and wealth; in the healthy and the dying, who believed that you were the resurrection and the life. In all these people I found you. Now I know that a church is only a building unless you live in the lives of those who come to worship. Acts of worship in our churches are only rituals without meaning unless those who perform them are filled with, and yearn, for your presence. Be present, Lord, in our churches and places of worship, especially in the minds and hearts of the young, so that they see beyond external actions and reach out in love to those around them in whom they see your abiding presence.

I am a weak person

I long for the inner peace you are always writing about. But I feel weak and worthless because I always give in to mastur-

bation. I pray that I will be strong enough to resist, but it is of little use. I am very happily married, and need your prayers and advice.

FRANK

As I have said time and again to people like you, it is important that you forgive yourself. All you can do is your best. God, as your Father, does not expect anything more. He would not be a loving Father if he did. The danger is that you can be so obsessed by this weakness that you are oppressed by it. It becomes '*the* thing' which dominates your life. It destroys your self-esteem and your happiness.

Frank, you and I live in a wounded world. None of us is perfect. St Paul's words will help you and others like you: 'I cannot understand my own behaviour. I fail to carry out the things I want to do, and I find myself doing the very things I hate. In my inmost self I dearly love God's Law, but I can see that my body follows a different law that battles against the law which my reason dictates. This is what makes me a prisoner of that law of sin which lives inside my body' (Romans 7:15–20)

There are worse sins, Frank, than those of the body. What about the rest of your life? Are you a generous and caring person? Are you a loving husband and father? How important is it for you to be God's friend? Do you really believe that he understands and forgives you? Do you want to live in the present moment? If so, then be gentle with yourself. In that way you will find inner peace of mind and heart.

❦ **FATHER**, you forgive my sins because you love me. I know that if I do not love myself for who and what I am, then I cannot love you. There are times when the only reason I have for loving myself is that you love me. You created me, and set me to live in a world damaged by sin of which I am a part. You do not love me because I am good and do your will in everything. You love and heal me because I am weak, and left to my own resources I would fail you in all that I am and do. You sent your son, Jesus, to be the loving doctor, who would heal my wounds. He is the good shepherd who carries me as his wounded lamb on his shoulders because I would not have the strength to walk alone. Teach me to be determined in the future to try to be strong and do your will, but when I fall, help me to remember that you love me still.

Now for the Good News

For as long as I can remember I have always felt lonely because I knew instinctively that my parents never really wanted me. They never showed me any affection. The only time they noticed me was to correct me. My home was an unhappy one with voices always raised in argument. It frightened me, and I drew in on myself. I tried to hide away from my brothers and sisters even in my own home. They called me the 'scared rabbit', not knowing how much they were hurting me. I hated school, never making any friends and lived in a fantasy world of my own making. As soon as I could I left home, and the room I could afford soon became my prison. Do you know how destructive loneliness can be? Well, I was lonely deep down inside of me. I went to church every Sunday, but avoided all contact with anyone who tried to make contact with me. Quite by accident one Sunday afternoon I came to an El Shaddai Healing Service. I had nothing better to do!

Then it all happened. You and your team prayed over me. In your sermon you seemed to believe that God loved you. I wanted that for myself too, and that is exactly what I got. You told me, 'May God the Father's love fill your heart today.' And it did. I have never looked back since. I have made many real friends. Loneliness is banished out of my life. I'm sorry it didn't happen to me before my parents died, but I was fifty-four the day I came to that healing service, and I have since been living my youth through friends. I have found my Father. Isn't he just wonderful?

MARY

❦ **FATHER**, I thank you this day for all my family and friends. Without them I would feel lonely and unwanted. In the times when I need to be alone with you, the memory of who they are, and what they mean to me warms my heart. They are your gift to me. I thank you for your Holy Spirit, which makes me realise that you are my Father who cares for me at every moment of my life. I pray today for all those who feel lonely that they too may experience the gift of a loving family. May their lives be enriched by friendship which dispels their loneliness, and makes them aware of their value to others, and to themselves. Show your love to those who have never really known you, and make them realise that you are their Father from whom all friendship flows.

Am I being punished for my sins?

Four months ago I had major surgery for a complete new knee joint. Something appears to have gone wrong and I am depressed by the fear that I shall never walk again. Is this because of some sin I have committed in the past for which God is punishing me?

JOHN

Nonsense. God doesn't punish us for our sins. He forgives us. We punish ourselves mainly by not believing in a loving God who wants us healthy and happy. The trouble with the operation is probably because of something in your knee joint which has not responded to treatment *as yet*. I say *as yet* because you and I are going to pray that everything is going to go right from now on.

John, you must be happy and at peace within yourself. God loves you. Never lose sight of that great uplifting truth. How can you be depressed if you let that light shine on your life? A peaceful person is much better equipped for physical 'healing' (curing) than someone who is not at peace within himself. Be patient with yourself. For your medicine take a large measure of hope whenever you feel the pain in your knee or your heart. It will transform you into a new person. A silly old knee joint is not going to upset your peace and happiness. God will put it, and you, right on the road to health and healing.

❦ GOD OUR FATHER, slow to anger and swift to compassion, make me realise that you never punish me for my sins, but forgive me more readily than I am prepared to forgive myself. Your Son, Jesus, told us to forgive our neighbour only as we forgive ourselves, so that if I do not forgive myself, then I am unable to forgive my neighbour. You are not a severe judge who watches over our every action and writes down everything we do wrong. You want to be known for what you are, a loving, forgiving Father, who heals not punishes his children. I pray for all those so tortured by guilt that they have lost their sense of inner peace. May they know you as a loving God who heals all their ills and removes their guilt as far away as the East is from the West.

I killed my child

I desperately need to know how to forgive myself for violently injuring and killing my child. I would not have done it if I had been in my right mind. Through my prison sentence I have paid my debt to society for killing my son, but what of myself? I am still haunted by past memories so that I just cannot forgive myself. Please help me.

JIMMY

57

Your greatest punishment is your memory of what you did. This terrible thing happened in the past. As you say, you have paid your debt to society, but what about the debt to yourself? You achieve nothing, in fact the opposite, if you let what happened haunt your memory. You must be feeling pretty awful, especially if, as the rest of your letter shows, you are a sensitive person who bitterly regrets what you have done.

Jimmy, you owe it to yourself to be at peace. Try to forgive the person you *were* when you did this so that you can become the kind of person God wants you to be. Jesus forgave the soldiers who crucified him and they, in turn, had to forgive themselves. So with you. Your child does not condemn you. Your injured son is the wounded Christ on the cross. If your child forgives you then you must forgive yourself. I pray for that gift for you. May it come soon.

❦ LORD JESUS, just after you were born, innocent children were killed in Bethlehem because of Herod's fear of losing his power. I pray for all those who have violently brought to an end the life of another human being. Put their minds at rest in the knowledge that you look after the one who died and is now in your loving care. Help them to go on living their lives as peacefully as possible and may they forgive themselves as they are forgiven by you. Let their memory be softened so that they no longer look on what they have done in the harsh light of day, but in the mellowness of your forgiveness in which you teach them to forgive themselves. Your forgiveness is the beginning of their new life as they leave the shadow of darkness and guilt behind them to walk in a land of light and forgiveness.

God does not hear my prayer

I cared for my ailing elder sister and brother for most of my life. I prayed to God that he would give me health and strength to make a worthwhile life of my own. Almost immediately after my brother's death I became crippled with arthritis. Does God wear ear-plugs and not listen to senior citizens who have given their lives to his Church and cause?

CINDY

I'm glad you asked that question. You are right to wonder if God is listening to you. After all, you have only one life to live and you have given the best part of it in caring for your brother and sister. You would expect some space for yourself now so that your future would be happy and healthy. A just reward? I would imagine so.

There is a danger, Cindy, that you could become bitter. Your saving grace is your remark about God having 'ear-plugs'. You obviously are blessed with a sense of humour, otherwise you would not have been able to cope with the limitations imposed on you by your arthritis. You are not being selfish even though some over-pious souls would tell you to grin and bear it! This is a cop-out, and solves nothing. You have to look at your painful situation and try to find an answer. It is not going to be easy.

Thank God you believe in God. Your faith will *gradually* help you to see things in a new and more mellow light. You have done well for those nearest to you. You have your sweet memories which you must not allow anyone to take from you. Allow others, caring people, whom I hope will come along, to care for you as you have done for others. As a senior citizen myself, I shall ask God to take out his ear-plugs next time you speak to him. We will see what happens.

❦ **FATHER**, it is hard for me, and for so many others, to believe that you listen to our prayers, because there are many times it seems that our words are falling on deaf ears. There have been numerous occasions when I asked and never received, sought and never found, knocked and the door was never opened. At such times, I needed a strong and deep faith to keep persevering in my attempts to have a conversation with you. It was at those times when I was tired of talking words to you and sat and listened patiently that you answered in a wonderful way which was beyond my hopes and dreams. May I remember those times when, on future occasions, I feel tempted to abandon prayer because I think that either you are no longer there, or you do not care or listen to me. Thank you, Father, for listening.

God only loves me when I am good

The way God has been, and is being, presented to me makes me very angry. I am told God loves me, but it does not seem so to me. We are loved only when we do not sin. If I knew I were safe in God's hands, even in sin, then I would feel sorrow and gratitude. I cannot love a God who does not accept my failures. Please comment.

MARY

God has no favourites. And if he had, they would be the sinners. This is what Jesus taught by his life style. He prefers the stray sheep ninety-nine times more than the others. I know where you got this false teaching from. I have heard it so often myself, and what a distortion it is of the Gospel. I suppose those who teach it *want* to keep us on the straight and narrow path which is a very restricted and untrue approach to life. They forget that sheep, especially lambs, get into all sorts of mischief. Jesus saw himself as the Good Shepherd, and told his followers, 'Feed my lambs . . . feed my sheep'!

When you stop loving God, it is not because of his failure to love you, but your own failure to love yourself. Jesus knows us, warts and all. You and I need to be told time and again that God loves us without ceasing because he has pity on us living in a world damaged by sin. The Church that preaches forgiveness of our sins can only do so in relation to its insistence that God never stops loving us for an instant. He is probably never closer to us than when we feel we have lost him by our behaviour. When we come to our senses like the Prodigal Son then we will realise that he loved us all the time, and wanted us back in his home where we really belong as his children whom he loves.

❦ HEAVENLY FATHER, I know you have no favourites, and each one is special to you. You love me as I am, and you are patient in waiting for me to change for the better because you want me to be free in being willing and wanting to change. Loving Father, change me and in my weakness be my strength, in my false security be my challenge, in my luke-warmness be a fire within me wanting things to be better, and in my life which is in a rut, raise me up so I can really live and face the future with grace and gallantry.

Remorse at abortion

When I was thirty-eight years old I became pregnant. The father of the baby made it clear that he did not want either of us. In a panic, I went into hospital and had an abortion. Since then I feel so overwhelmingly guilty, I cannot live with myself. I have a great self-hatred. What should I do?

ELIZABETH

The first thing you must do is to love and forgive yourself. This is what God wants you to do. It would be wrong to do otherwise. Abortion is wrong, but two wrongs won't make a right. Your guilt is killing your life, and God as your Father has given you life which you must try to live to the full.

The past is dead. You cannot bring your baby back. You have to learn to live in the present. It is never easy especially for those who have an abortion. As well as guilt you are obviously feeling bitter regret for what has happened and this can be a very negative, destructive emotion. It puts you back into the situation *before* the abortion. You look at it now in the cold light of day and you appreciate what a terrible thing it is, but you were in a panic at the time. If you knew *then* what you know *now* it would not have happened. You must put this behind you, and live calmly and peacefully.

Whenever, and if ever, you meet someone who is tempted to have an abortion you will be able to help them. You will become a saver of life, and what is more wonderful than that?

You have learned the hard and cruel way. Now begin to live a new life by loving yourself. God and your baby would want it no other way.

❦ **LORD JESUS**, lover of little children, I pray for all mothers who because of circumstances have had an abortion. The memory of what happened often brings with it the punishment of overpowering guilt and emotional upset which destroy that mothers's peace. Self-recrimination about the past will never bring the baby back. Soothe the minds and hearts of all mothers who suffer in this way, and may they know that their child is happy with you.

Am I really sorry?

My problem dates back to my teens, and I have now turned 70! It is the difference between 'attrition' and 'contrition' which has caused me endless worry. I go to confession regularly and wonder if my sorrow is sufficient for a good confession. What advice would you give me?

ALBERT

My advice is simple. No sorrow is sufficient or big enough to make up for our sin, none so little that God would choose to ignore it. The fact that you go to confession means that you believe God forgives your sin because he loves you. Don't work yourself into a spiritual frenzy trying to be sorry. If you do then you are looking on forgiveness from your approach rather than from God's. He is your loving Father after all.

Remember the story of the Prodigal Son. He came home not because he missed his father's love, but because he was physically hungry. The Father didn't worry about his son's motives. It was sufficient for him that his son came home. It was the Father's love that really mattered in the final analysis. Read the story (Luke 11:15–32). It will surely help you.

So, Albert, stop worrying. Come *home* in confession. It is where your Father wants to show his unchanging love for you. After all this is what matters where forgiveness of sin is concerned.

✢ LORD JESUS, I thank you that you gave your apostles the power to forgive sins in your name, and reconcile sinners to your Father, their neighbours and themselves. Even though time and again I have told you how sorry I am, yet I still persist in my waywardness. I ask you, Lord, in your goodness that you will continue to forgive my failings in the future, and set my mind at rest about my past. When you were on earth, you readily forgave sinners and encouraged them to live better lives. I pray that you will do the same for me so that I live in peace in my spirit, because I know that the abundance of your love makes up for my lack of sorrow.

Now for the Good News

For years I was crippled by migraine. I had to sit for hours in the dark with the most terrible pains in my head which nearly drove me out of my mind. I was also restless at night because when I went to sleep I had the most awful nightmares. These may seem trivial complaints to you, but they were not to me.

They had brought my life to a standstill. I had been to doctors and psychiatrists who tried their best to help me, but any relief was only temporary.

I was on the verge of despair when I came four years ago to an El Shaddai healing service which was all about loving God and loving yourself with a love which cast out fear. I realised for the first time in my life that I neither loved God nor myself. I was afraid of God. I felt he would punish me for my sins and so I said my prayers that I would live for as long as possible so as not to fall into his hands.

I could see how relaxed and happy everyone was at the service. I also realised that I did not think myself worthy enough to go to heaven so that eventually when I died I would go to hell. This was the source of my nightmares. Hell was real for me, heaven was for other people. As you laid hands on me you said quietly 'Peace be to you'. I experienced a peace which I cannot put into words. Since that day four years ago I have slept soundly without nightmares. Incidentally I never had another attack of migraine again.

BRENDA

❦ **FATHER**, you loved me even before I was formed in my mother's womb. It is your love for me which causes me to love myself as a reflection of your love which never comes to an end. Teach me never to fear you because in so doing, I will cloud over your light in my life and condemn myself to live in darkness. Your love for me is my only hope of loving myself and other people. Give me, I pray you, this love which casts out fear, and grant me the true freedom to live my life as you would have me do, a life free from fear and free to love.

I want employment

I have been unemployed for three years and it hurts. All I get through the post are rejection letters. Jesus said, 'Ask and you shall receive.' I have asked so often and so hard in my prayers, but he never answers. I feel depressed and abandoned.

TONY

I am not surprised at how low you feel. It is soul-destroying not to have your talents used in useful and constructive employment. You are suffering from one of the great diseases of our computerised consumer society. We priests never have to run the risk of being made redundant, or have to worry about where we will find the financial resources necessary to support ourselves and our families. It is only by receiving hundreds of letters from people in your situation, and trying to help them, that I have come to appreciate how depressed, worried and unwanted you must feel.

I hope you find suitable employment, Tony. It may be small comfort to you but I shall pray for you and for others in a similar situation. Read Luke 18:1–8. It will show you how to pray in your situation. Knock *louder* so that God cannot *but* hear you. If he does not seem to, then have a good argument with him. Don't take it lying down and go away feeling beaten and alone. I never do.

In the ministry of inner healing I am not afraid to *challenge* God. It has had a wonderful effect on my faith, and the results that prayer achieves. Don't just *ask*, be prepared to *shout*. Don't *knock* on the door, *bang* on it and wake up the whole household. Tell him, 'It's me, Tony. I am your friend, I *need* a job *now*!' Wait and see what happens. Keep in touch.

❦ HEAVENLY FATHER, you have decreed that by the sweat of our brows we are to earn our daily bread. I thank you that all through my life you have given me the health, skill, opportunity and motivation to provide not only for myself but also for those whom I love and are dependent on me. In a spirit of gratitude and sympathy, I turn to you in prayer on behalf of those whose labour has never been sought, and who still at the eleventh hour stand idle at the market place. Call them out, Lord, for some task which you want them to perform which you have found for them and give them a sense of self-assurance and confidence as they begin a new life in which their value is recognised. Make our society more aware of their needs so that leaders of industry think not so much of profit as the dignity and rights of people to engage in work which fulfills the purpose for which they were created.

Christmas without my loving husband

I dread this Christmas. My husband and I were happily married for forty years until he died in September. My children and their families will share with me but I dread the thought of my husband, Tom, not being there. Am I being selfish?

MABEL

You are not being in the least selfish. It is natural and perfectly normal for you to grieve. Christmas will not be the same without your husband. You can't put forty happy Christmases behind you, and pretend they did not happen. They are part of you.

This year you have to face a new experience, and you do not know how you are going to cope. You are blessed to have your family around you. Others are not so fortunate. Many people have rarely ever known a happy Christmas. The joy of others highlights their own sense of loneliness.

Mabel, try not to be lonely, and be glad that you have known so many happy times with Tom. Christmas is a time for remembering the past, so concentrate on the good things you shared together. Thank God for them. You will have your quiet weep, but your faith that you will be with your husband again will give you the strength to cope. Jesus said,

66

'Blessed are those who mourn, they shall be comforted.' Your faith that love never ends in death will be your anchor. Talk to your husband as you always did. He is not absent, even if you cannot see him. He is with you and your children in spirit. His love lives on in you and your children. They are sensitive to your feelings and they will help you see Christmas through in many little kindnesses. Accept their love. It is part of God's love and Tom's for you.

❧ **LORD JESUS**, you came on earth for everyone so that no one would be excluded from your all-embracing love. Inspire me with the same spirit of generosity so that I may always remain open, especially to those who have hurt me in the past, or towards whom I have nurtured feelings of resentment. May this, and every day, be like Christmas as you inspire me to bring peace and reconciliation to all those whom I meet in my journey through life.

I cannot make friends

I cannot seem to relate to anyone. I am completely wrapped up in myself and cannot reach out to others. What can I do?

MIRIAM

You need friends. You know that but yet you don't seem able to make any. The fault could be in yourself. Strange as it may seem, this is my advice to you. The first person to be friends with is yourself. As your own friend you realise how vital it is for you to have friends. You need them, and they need you. This is the first step in seeking friendship. You are not friends with yourself if you are negative, over-critical, or depressing in your outlook. If you are your own friend you are positive, appreciative and look on the bright side of life. You know you have a lot to give in friendship so you are generous in your approach to others because you want the other person to be as happy as you are. You don't feel threatened by friends, and so you are not an 'even scales' person who wants an equal return for what she gives to her friend. You are not afraid of being hurt and when you are, you are not tempted to draw back into your protective shell. You are not a 'bunker' person. Neither will you manipulate people. Friendships cannot be planned. They happen.

I am very happy. I want you to be happy too. We have never met, Miriam, but I want you to know that you are my friend, and when we meet we will both know how beautiful our friendship is.

❦ LORD JESUS, you sought friends in your life to share your missions and your moments of your deepest joy and sorrow. Without friendship, inner peace is impossible. I thank you that my life has been blessed with true deep lasting friendships. The poorest person in the world is the one who has no friends. I am today what people have offered me of themselves in friendship. I pray for all those who are lonely today with no one to share their lives, or to notice their comings and goings in a world which takes no account of them. Open my heart to them so that with a smile, a gentle touch, a little act of kindness, I may lighten their darkness, and make them aware that it is you who is smiling and being their friend through me.

Afraid of growing old

I am afraid of growing old. I am absolutely terrified of ending up in an old people's home and living like a vegetable. How can I rid myself of this fear?

DAVID

As we grow older we are more concerned with death, rather than with life. What you need to concentrate on, David, is that we are all *'growing.'* We *mature* with age. There is no situation in life, whatever our age, when we are not capable of growing. In all growth, especially in suffering, we become more human, alive and Christian. There is no age for dying or growing old. I know many 'old' people who are more alive than so-called young people. It is all a question of outlook.

David, the future is hidden from your eyes. No one knows what their tomorrow will be. Enjoy life today. It is all you have, and you could not ask for anything better. I feel younger today than I did twenty years ago because I am so fulfilled. No matter what our age is we need to borrow the eyes of a child so that we can look at the world in awe and wonder. All the aches in your creaking joints are growing-points. They mean you are alive! If you live life to the full today then you will be better prepared for what tomorrow may bring. So, David, do not be afraid of growing old. Rather be afraid of not growing young.

❦ **HEAVENLY FATHER**, as I become increasingly aware that I am growing old through the signs of age which mark my body and slow down my movements, I pray that you will lead me gently through this stage of my life. Increase my awareness of you rather than allowing myself to be preoccupied with my increasing mental and bodily fatigue. Deepen my faith and trust in you that all will be well as long as I keep my eyes steadfastly fixed on you. Mellow my memory so that it thinks only of those things in life which brought me to a deeper understanding of my loved ones, of you and of myself. May I live each day to the full to savour it as wine that has matured with age, and may I share each drop and each moment with you.

Prayer is a duty

Prayers for me are a duty. They are something to be 'got in.' If I don't say them I feel guilty and yet no matter how many prayers I say, my life doesn't change for the better. Am I praying wrongly?

MABEL

Sorry, Mabel, but if you are not changing for the better then you are not praying. You are saying prayers, but they are words which do not flow from your mind and heart. Prayer is thinking about God while loving him. If we think of God as he is, as our Father, then we will love him. We can do this in silence; this is a special form of prayer. If we use words, then this is vocal prayer.

I love just to sit and think about God rather than use a whole lot of words. In fact, I am often lost for words because they cannot express what I am feeling deep inside. I don't want to 'get my words in', as if this is prayer. This is a pagan attitude. At least that is what Jesus said: 'In your prayers, do not babble as the pagans do, for they think that by using many words they will make themselves heard' (Matthew 6:7).

Mabel, try a new way. This evening when you have read this reply, fold the paper up, close your eyes. Don't worry about trying to think 'holy thoughts'! Just sit there quietly. Be patient and listen, God will speak to you. In return you may want to speak to him. This is a conversation, this is prayer.

❦ HOLY SPIRIT, without you no prayer is possible. Because I am weakened by sin there are a thousand and one things which so distract me that I find that I have lost the desire to pray. Prayer becomes a duty for me which I feel I have to fulfil, and so I get my prayers 'in', prayers which are just words and do not flow from my heart. I know you have come at other times and filled me with your presence as I listened to what you spoke to me. My listening was much more important than anything I could say to you. So I ask you to slow me down and encourage me to sit and listen to your still small voice when my world is hushed and your peace is all I seek. This I know is my deepest prayer which comes from my heart to which you have brought your peace.

Now for the Good News

I have some good news that you might like to share with your congregations or your weekly readers. A number of years ago, I suffered from agoraphobia. It was severe and resulted in me having to give up my place at university and confining myself to the house for about three years. As I was in my early twenties at this time, you can imagine the effect this was having upon me. At one time I thought that I was going to remain in the house for ever, until I was visited by a friend of my mother's. This friend was a member of a charismatic prayer group and when she called she brought her brother, who is a priest, with her. She had come to cut my hair, but before she got her scissors out she asked me if I would like her and her brother to pray with me. I agreed to this.

Within a few days of being prayed with, I felt an urge to go outside again. This was still very difficult for me, and it took a lot of prayer, and help from a wonderful social worker and a psychologist, to help me to overcome the terrible feelings of panic and to venture back into the real world again and to escape from my secure, but prison-like, home.

I was prayed with in July 1983. Within six months I was attending our local prayer group, the one that our family friend belonged to. I started to attend Mass regularly again after Easter in 1984. I started a course of study in July 1984 which led me to returning to university as a full-time student in September 1985. I graduated in July 1989 with a BA (Hons.) 2.1, and I then went to England to do a one year teacher training course in September of that year. I returned to Northern Ireland to take up a temporary teaching post in September 1990, and have just received my first permanent post (teaching posts are few and far between in Northern Ireland!).

I graduated this summer with an MA in English after following a three year, part-time course of study.

I have a lot to be thankful for and I owe it all to God, the love of Jesus, and the power of the Holy Spirit. My illness has brought me into the sort of relationship with God that would have been previously unimaginable to me, and I have received a sense of peace and happiness that is at times overwhelming, but in the nicest of ways. Although I would not wish the horrors of agoraphobia on my worst enemy, I am glad that my life has taken the paths that it has taken.

RICHARD

❦ **O GOD**, whose mercy is boundless and whose gifts are without end, help me always to thank you for everything that your loving power has bestowed on me. Make me realise that my desire to thank you is itself your gift, and that my thankfulness is never-ending because your love is never-failing.

I am ashamed of my body

I am ashamed of my body. Ever since I was a child I always thought I was too skinny. I was afraid to go swimming for example. I have never lost this sense of embarrassment and it is ruining my life. Why do I think like this?

STEVE

Others have taught you to think like this. It is not your fault. Because of this false teaching, the physical importance and appearance of the body have been grossly exaggerated. This has led to all sorts of excesses, including making sins of the flesh *the* only sins that matter. This wrong approach ignores the sins of the spirit and emotions like jealousy, hatred and so on, which are equally, if not more, destructive of you as a person.

Steve, your body is part of you just like everything else which goes to make you up as a person. It is you as a person that counts. You look after your body because it is important to you. It is the temple of the Holy Spirit. This is why you must not eat or drink excessively because it ruins your health. Sufferers from eating disorders please note: How you look to others and to outward appearances doesn't really matter. Have a healthy spirit in a healthy body and then you will be a healthy person. Healing is, after all, a health-giving exercise.

❦ **LORD JESUS**, you were stripped naked in public and nailed to a cross. You turned that scene of shame into a triumph of love so that the crucifix is forever a sign of your victory over sin and evil. May I always respect my body as a gift given to me by my Father, using food and drink for its nourishment, neither eating nor drinking to excess nor eating too little, both of which would damage it. May I never be ashamed of your gift realising that it is how we see it, and not how other people look at us, which is important.

I was jilted

Just before we were due to be married, my fiancé called the wedding off. A few months later he married someone else. I feel rejected and unwanted. I just cannot put my life together again and don't feel I shall ever get over it, even though it happened a year ago. Can you give me any advice?

CAROL

You are probably a very fortunate person, even though you do not see it that way just now. I dread to think what it would have been like if you had married, and later on found you were most unhappy together. At least your former fiancé had the courage to break off the engagement, whatever his motivation. This is not much consolation to you now, but when the troubled waters settle down you will see things more clearly.

Of course, you feel rejected and unwanted. You have just

been through a most traumatic and unnerving episode in your life. It is a kind of emotional death, and so you grieve. You will go through all the emotions of hating your ex-fiancé and his wife. Hating yourself is probably the most destructive aftermath of such an emotional breakdown for you. You will go through anger, cutting yourself off from others because you feel you are soiled, a 'second' in a store. Never mind what the neighbours think. What you need is patience with yourself, and time and space to cope with the new situation.

The dawn will eventually break through the darkness. You will grow through all the pain you experience just now. I won't give you any 'holy' advice. You will emerge a new person. God will see to that. He will show you the way ahead.

❦ LORD JESUS, you knew the pain of being deserted by those whom you called your friends. We all suffer the pain of rejection in one form or another. It is hardest to bear when it is someone special in whom we placed our most treasured hopes for our future life. I pray today for all those whose love for someone they hold dear is not returned, or is even spurned. May they be filled with an understanding of their hurt so that it will help them to grow through it and not see it as a reason for thinking less of themselves. Fill their thoughts not of the darkness of the pain of yesterday, but of the dawn of tomorrow in which they will continue their journey in search of friendship, peace and fulfilment.

Bullied by my sister

When I was young, my elder sister always bullied me. She never gave me credit for anything, but made me feel inferior and guilty in her presence. Even now, fifty years later, I still have the same feelings towards her. I am still the younger sister in my attitude, and I resent it. Any advice?

BETTY

74

This is more typical of what happens in family life than we choose to believe. There is no easy remedy. Brothers and sisters can be very violent with each other, and never seem to lose the elder brother or sister approach. We shrink in the other person's presence when they are around. I remember the day I beat my elder brother at tennis. It was a traumatic and liberating experience for us both. I became free from then on to be myself, and we became real friends. He was himself and I was myself.

Betty, you have to grow up, and so must your sister. You are not children any more. If she won't let you be yourself then it seems that you have no option but to walk away. If not, then every time you meet the battle will be renewed, and no one is the victor in this fruitless form of encounter. You have to love yourself and this requires space and freedom. Friends will give them to you, and your brothers and sisters should do the same, but it doesn't always work out that way. It is true that you can choose your friends, but not your family. Give your sister an opportunity to be your friend. If she does not want it that way, then leave her in her childish ways, but you must walk free with your friends if you want to grow as a person. You can still love your sister, but don't ever let her bully you into not being yourself. That approach is for children who never grow up.

❦ JESUS, you blessed the human family by choosing to spend thirty years in the family home at Nazareth. Bless all families today so that they may live together in love, peace and harmony. I pray for all families in which there is discord between brothers and sisters which damages them as persons, and blights their lives. Friendship requires time and space in which to grow in a better understanding of the other person. The present family situation with all its distractions and turmoil does not give members of families this opportunity to discover each other as persons. I pray to you, Lord, that you enter our homes and fill them again with your peace as once you did at Nazareth.

Quiet until he drinks

My husband is a gentle, loving person until he gets a drink. Then his whole personality changes. The children are scared of him and I fear that when they leave home that is the last we shall see of them. I feel so powerless to do anything. Should I remain quiet and hope for the best?

JOAN

When excessive drinking comes in the front door of a home, then love disappears out the back. Drink takes over and the home becomes a house, even a prison, for those who have to live with the consequences. Everyone suffers, including the one addicted to alcohol, and unfortunately, by and large, we have turned a blind eye to it in the Church. Drink is as destructive of a Christian home as poverty. In poverty we need material goods to live a human existence, but in excessive drinking we destroy the sharing together in harmony which is so necessary for family life.

Joan, you are not powerless. You must do something positive to help your children, your husband and yourself. You need to talk to your husband, but only when he is sober, and never after a row or the morning after the night before. Ask God to put the right words on your lips. Don't make your husband feel guilty because if you do, he will probably defend himself. Drink is, after all, an addiction just like gambling or any other hobby which takes up an excessive amount of the time which should be spent with the family.

You need to try and discover why your husband feels the need to drink so much. This is his escape route, but from what? His violence is probably due to frustration, and he is taking it out on himself as much as you and the children.

Keep in touch with me. Next time I have an El Shaddai service in your area bring him with you. I would like to share with you both what God can do for you. He wants you all to live at peace in your home. This is what Christian family life is all about.

✝ **LORD JESUS CHRIST**, you showed us the value of so many things when used in moderation and on the right occasion. Aware of the terrible consequences to individuals and their families when used to excess, I pray that I shall always use alcohol in such a way that it never controls me. I pray for all families who have suffered emotionally, physically and spiritually because of alcoholism. May this abuse in families be brought under control and the scars it has caused be healed. Increase a better understanding of alcoholism and its causes in our Church and world so that we treat its victims with gentleness and firmness. Lord, through your love for families protect them from the dangers of alcoholism, and bring peace into their homes.

Does the Church believe in healing?

Our parish priest refuses to anoint anyone who is not physically ill. He says that the Church doesn't approve of any other form of healing. What should I say to him?

THOMAS

Your parish priest is talking only about the Sacrament of the Sick which is more or less specifically concerned with physical illness. It is a healing sacrament administered by the priest alone, but is not the only form of healing. There are countless other forms of healing which the Church has gradually neglected over the centuries. Christian healing concerns itself with every aspect of a person's life. We are wounded, not only in our bodies, but also in our emotions, spirit, soul and in situations which damage us to such an extent that we become less human, less Christian, less a person.

Healing for Jesus was of the whole person. The Sacrament of the Sick by definition is limited to physical illness. Today there is a whole new understanding of what Christian healing is all about, and our Church documents are talking about healing in a much broader way. Jesus healed fear, guilt, worry, anxiety and myriad other things which adversely affect our lives. This is what we do in our El Shaddai ministry. We stand together with the Sacraments of the Sick and Reconciliation as a means of helping or healing people in other ways in different aspects of their lives. We encourage people to believe in God as their personal Father who loves them and wants to heal them and make them whole.

I shall send you the El Shaddai Publications list of seven books and nine tapes which I have produced. I hope they answer all your questions and will surely help your parish priest to lose his fear of healing. Healing in its many forms changes our lives because it is God alone who heals us. All of us, priests and people, need all the healing we can get.

❦ **LORD JESUS**, in every situation you are healing your people from everything which injures them as persons. You healed the sick, gave sight to the blind, and even raised the dead to life. When you sent your apostles on their first mission, you told them to cure the sick, raise the dead, cleanse the lepers and cast out devils. You said you would be with them always because they were your Church, and this is what you wanted them to do. You promised to be with your Church always and you are with it today whenever it heals in your name. I thank you for all the healing of mind, body and spirit which takes place today in your name, in every corner of the world. May I encourage everyone to believe in your willingness and power to heal your people, and may your healing mission grow as we witness to your name in a world which sorely needs your healing love and presence.

Why do I get so angry?

I feel very strongly about moral matters and I get angry very easily with people who don't seem to care. Is anger always evil? What do you think?

ALEX

Anger can be a very liberating and necessary emotion. Jesus was justifiably angry with the money-changers in the temple. For him it was a moral issue. No one had done anything about it for years and so the temple entrance had degenerated into a market. He drove them out of his Father's house. He was angry with the Pharisees and called them 'hypocrites' and a 'brood of vipers.' Not very nice language, but Jesus thought it was justified by the situation and people with whom he was confronted. They did not practise what they preached.

Alex, I get angry myself when I feel frustrated by people who, in the presence of violence, walk by on the other side. They support violence by silence. I have been in violent political situations where silence by the Church has been its condemnation.

Justifiable anger is the antidote to violence. God uses our anger to heal us. I have seen people angry with God because of a tragedy which has erupted in their lives. The sudden death of their child, the terminal cancer which has struck down their beloved wife or husband causes anger. It is good to be angry with God and to ask him why us. He doesn't want us to take things lying down as if we were fatalists who don't believe that God can do anything about it. He can use our anger to heal us, and when the storm is over he will bring us his peace. The temple will no longer be full of money-changers. It will be once again a house of prayer where we will find our peace.

✠ **LORD JESUS CHRIST**, by word and action you have shown us that anger is justifiable on certain occasions. In every situation during your lifetime, your anger was directed at those who abused their position and who deserved everything you said and did. You saw anger as a necessary human emotion with which to express yourself, but you controlled your anger and did not let it control you. I ask you, Lord, that you give me the gift of using and controlling my anger as you did yours. May I never use it in a way that takes me over to the detriment of others and myself. Guide and strengthen me so that I never shirk my responsibilities in opposing violence and injustice and, when the waves of anger pass, send me your peace to still my spirit, knowing that what I said and did is what you would have done in similar circumstances.

Now for the Good News

My husband, John, and I had a very blessed and happy time at the El Shaddai annual conference in May. Afterwards we travelled to France for a short holiday before returning to our home in Scotland. After a few days, John complained of a pain in his chest, so we came back to England earlier than anticipated.

As soon as we left the harbour John had a massive heart attack and I took over the driving of the car. I pulled down a slip road from the M25. We were both very frightened. John, because of all the pain, and myself for having to watch and trying to cope as best I could to get help as quickly as possible.

What happened next is what I call a miracle. Down the slip road, in minutes, came an ambulance which I flagged down. It had two paramedics on board who kept John alive until they got him to hospital. After days of intensive care we were told by the hospital authorities that John's heart had not been damaged in any way and there was no scarring. He told me that he was at peace throughout it all because when you prayed with him in Scarborough and laid your hands on him, you said, 'Do not worry; everything will be all right.' And how right you were.

I believe that the prayers of the people at that very special El Shaddai conference saved my husband's life. It is for us a miracle and a proof of our Lord's healing today in our lives. Thank you. Our faith is strengthened and we have a new outlook on life.

JANET AND JOHN

❦ **LORD JESUS**, healer of people, I thank you for the many miracles of healing you have worked, not only during your lifetime on earth but also in our world today. I bless you for the many instances of your special intervention which have changed every aspect of people's lives, whether physical, spiritual or emotional. Through your healing, my own life has been changed in so many ways, some of them hidden from me at present. Awaken in me an awareness of all you have done, and are doing for me, so that I may proclaim my belief to everyone that you live and heal all those who believe in your name.

I am a worrier

I am 71 years of age and have been bedevilled by anxiety for most of my life. I worry about pain and death and wonder if I really believe in God. I long to be free and yet I am a prisoner. Please, what do I do?

BEN

Anxiety or worry is most destructive. You are right to say that even though you want to be free, nevertheless, anxiety is preventing you from living a full, human life. This is why

81

Jesus said we were not to worry. Worry adds nothing to life but rather takes from it. Ben, I cannot stop you worrying. Only you yourself can do that with God's help. I want you, however, to ask yourself some straightforward questions to which you should give honest answers as best you can.

What do you worry about most? Death? But this worry prevents you from enjoying life. Are your worries really justified? When did they start to cripple your lifestyle? Do you realise that worry is one of the worst pains you can inflict on yourself? Do you cause pain to those you love by your worrying? Do you give yourself and your situation the benefit of the light of hope? Do you know that shadows are longer than reality in the evening time? Are you a sunrise or a sunset person?

Worry makes you into a grave digger for your own burial. You are not meant to live in a cemetery. Come away into a garden and share the joy of being alive with other people. If you want to live with your worry then there is little anyone can do to help you. You are like someone who has never learned to swim because he is afraid the water is too cold. Come on in – into life. It is not as cold as you think. Christ will show you the way to be free and how to enjoy your freedom.

❦ **LORD JESUS**, worry is destroying my life, and bringing it to a stand-still. It fills the past with guilt, and the future with fear. I worry about everything and it has become so much a part of me that I am unable to feel comfortable in myself unless I have something to worry about. Lord Jesus, you lived in very frightening circumstances surrounded as you were by prejudice, intrigue and hypocrisy, yet you never lost your peace. Even on the cross as you were dying you surrendered the rest of your life to your Father. Put your spirit of peace within me so that I leave the past to your mercy, the future to your loving care, and live in the present moment free from worry and full of the joy and challenge of living my life one day at a time.

Christmas is too commercialised

I feel very hurt that we seem to have lost the spirit of Christmas. I am fed up to the teeth with all the carols coming at me from every shop and supermarket. Is this commercialism wrong?

DENIS

I know how you feel. Christmas is over-commercialised, but then so is Lourdes. We still go there on pilgrimage even though we run the gauntlet of all the shops peddling their wares under the shelter of a religious umbrella. Our Lady appeared to a peasant girl and gave the world the inspiration to come there to pray. Lourdes is the peace of the grotto, and the crib is the true meaning of Christmas despite all the ballyhoo.

The whole idea of God's Son being born in a stable unlocks the human heart and mind so that at least for a few short days we believe in peace and hope for a world stressed by violence and despair. It is a time for the family, and for giving help to others less fortunate than ourselves. Yesterday in a supermarket I watched wide-eyed children gazing at three huge cuddly mechanical teddy bears singing carols. I was fascinated by the children, but I was also entranced myself. There is a child in all of us.

Carols without the crib are meaningless. We know that behind the carols, however sentimental and commercial, there is a story. I believe it and that is why I shall kneel before a crib and thank God for giving us Christmas.

❦ FATHER, faith is a precious gift which gives me new insights into the really wonderful things in our world hidden behind the facade of glitz and glamour. Because we are human there are times when we obscure even great spiritual events. Today, I thank you, Father, that your Son came to our world into a humble loving home; that he grew to manhood as a simple carpenter in the village shop of Nazareth; that he shared our life with all its sorrows and joy. May I borrow his eyes this day, and look on my world with his vision of peace, and see the glory of your beauty which is hidden except to those who look with eyes of faith.

I want to be great

I have always wanted to be rich and powerful, but I never made it. I envy people who have. Is power-seeking all that wrong?

ROGER

The greatest thing you can do in your life is to try to discover who you really are, and then to be yourself. When you are yourself, then you can be poor or rich, powerful or of no consequence in the world's eyes, but you can cope because you are being true to yourself. It is part of you. You are not changed by power or the lack of it. This is the rock on which your personality is based. People obsessed with power are not at peace within themselves.

Roger, when you are yourself you may not wield power, but more importantly, you will have a great *influence* on people's lives without even being aware of it. You will be amazed at what passes over from your life into the lives of other people, some of whom you may have met only casually. They are enriched by who and what you are.

The people who have influenced me were never powerful people. They have been the 'ordinary' folk who were nobodies in the world's eyes. Take John, for example, who died many years ago. He was an alcoholic who came to work for me in the garden. Now there was a powerful person in the right sense of the word. John was, for me, the wounded Christ. Christ's power is not of this world. The Church and its members need to follow him if we want to influence people, but sadly we don't. Power is our hypnotic, destructive drug.

Roger, you have gone wrong. As a Christian you should have sought the kingdom of God first. This kingdom is within you. It is there that you will find the power of peace, happiness and fulfilment. It is not too late to start the search.

❦ **LORD JESUS**, friend of the poor and under privileged, you gave us the perfect example of what our attitude to rank and power should be. You said if we wanted to be fulfilled then we should seek the Kingdom of your Father first and everything else would fall into place. Power, as the world understands it, was something you avoided, and you told your followers that if they were to be like you they were not to court secular power, because your kingdom was not of this world. Guide my footsteps so that I never stray from the true path because you are my only way to the Father whom I wish to serve in my life in all that I say and do.

No love in our marriage

I have been married for 15 years. Sex has been the main thing which my husband wants from our marriage. We have not grown together as adult people and I feel we are missing out. Am I right?

PATRICIA

Sex without a personal relationship is a form of prostitution. Sex is an expression of love or it is nothing at all. Instead of preaching about the use of sex in marriage, we priests should emphasise the true meaning of love as expressed in the context of husband and wife sharing their lives together. Marriage which has sex as its main platform is doomed to failure.

Patricia, I don't think your husband has grown up. He has not progressed beyond the sex stage. He is an older adolescent who is unable to share at a deep personal level.

Shared love involves all forms of personal *intimate* relationships which are not sexual. There is a laughter born of sharing in marriage which is beautifully Christian.

Yes, you are missing out, and I feel sorry for you. I don't know what advice to give you because this is a very delicate problem. I would like to have a heart-to-heart discussion with your husband. It would have to be a very sensitive approach on my part, otherwise our conversation would soon come to an abrupt end and he would tell me to mind my own business. He needs healing because otherwise your marriage will not last much longer: I'm surprised that it has survived 15 years. Tell him what I said, and we will see what happens. Thank you for sharing your pain.

❦ HEAVENLY FATHER, you created man and woman, blessed their union, and gave them the earth for their heritage. Your Son, Jesus, looked on this union as something very special and personal. It was to show his unique respect for husband and wife that he turned water into wine for a young married couple at their wedding feast. He saw marriage as essentially a relationship in which the husband and wife grow together by sharing every aspect of their lives. They were not to regard it solely in sexual terms. Send your Spirit into my heart this day so that I may look on marriage as you did. I pray for all those couples whose love has grown cold. May they rekindle their relationships, and realise that marriage is a complete sharing in which they grow as persons who have chosen to share their lives together.

Is there life after death?

How can you be so sure that there is another life after death. I have not got a faith like that. I am not sure at all. Why doesn't God give us more signs of the afterlife? Am I wrong to doubt?

JOSEPHINE

86

Of course, I'm not sure. No one is. Belief that makes for certainty is not belief at all. We *hope* that there is another life and this hope is based on our belief that Jesus rose from the dead. It is the anchor of our faith and an anchor is the symbol the Church uses for hope. 'If Jesus did not rise again', says St Paul, 'then we are the most unfortunate people in the world' (1 Corinthians 15:19).

The Apostle, Thomas, doubted in the resurrection of Jesus. He became the one to profess his belief in clear terms of 'my Lord and my God' when Jesus appeared especially to him to convince him of the great truth of life after death. Thomas's doubting was a prelude to his act of faith. So don't worry, Josephine, about your doubting. This shows that you want to believe in life after death because it is so precious to you. I am distrustful of people who never have doubts about anything in their religion. Doubt can be a very healthy spiritual experience, when it is part of our pilgrimage in faith.

And as for signs, Jesus said that the only sign that will be given is that of Jonah in the whale's belly (Matthew 12:39). We don't need people coming back from the dead to tell us what it is like on the 'other side'. This smacks of spiritualism. No, I don't need those kinds of signs. Jesus, risen from the dead, is my sign, my faith and my hope in life after death. Josephine, if we don't meet in this life, then I look forward, in hope, to meeting you in the next.

❦ LORD JESUS, you who said you were the resurrection and the life, so that all who believe in you will never die because they will share your risen life, help me to believe in your promise and to live by it. There are times in my life when I doubted because death seemed so final in the lives of my parents, brother and sister. I believe that I shall see them again where there will be no more mourning or weeping. I believe also that you raised Lazarus from the dead, and that your own resurrection is my only hope of life after death.

May my belief in eternal life as my destiny conquer my fear of death and dying.

I am in a second marriage

I am thirty-five years old. When I was twenty, I had a most unfortunate marriage which, if I had stayed in it, would have destroyed me. Later I fell in love with Jeremy and we married, but my annulment process fell through because of a Church legal hitch. Jeremy is everything a good Christian husband should be. The Church tells me I am living in sin, but I just cannot see it like that. Does God reject us too?

JENNIFER

Certainly not. God loves you and you obviously love him. You love the Church too, otherwise you wouldn't have tried to get annulment. There are hundreds like you today, but this is small consolation. You want to be, and to feel, right with the Church. In your heart there is a conflict between the rules of the Church, and God's love for you as a Father. There is no easy answer and I am not going to enter the controversy in which grave misunderstanding might take place. This is causing enough pain today to so many people and I don't want to add to it.

It is surely asking too much of anyone either to stay in a marriage situation which is destructive of you as a person, or to live like a nun for the rest of your life. It was never your vocation, and it is not now. Just as in your disastrous marriage, so also the present situation as regards the Church's law is preventing you from living a full Catholic life in peace. What is God's will for you? It is obvious from what you write that your love for Jeremy is a source of healing for you and you see God's love is in it. To say otherwise would be for you to fly in the face of truth. To see Church law as something independent of the love of God is to ignore the Gospel in which Jesus said that love is the fulfilling of all laws.

Cases like yours, Jennifer, cause great heartache in the lives of so many people. There is little point in acknowledging the problem unless we do everything in our power to find a solution. Marriage *is* under attack today, which tends to make the attitude of some legally-orientated people more unbending in their upholding of the law irrespective of the harm it does to peoples lives. It is a testing time for you, Jennifer, and for the Church. We are in this together, and we want God to be in it too.

❦ **HEAVENLY FATHER**, I pray for all those who are caught up in Church law and who because of it are unable to be accepted fully as members of the Church community. Be with them in their emotional and spiritual distress and let them know that you have never withdrawn your love from them. Set them free from all thoughts of being misunderstood, abandoned or rejected as in their situation they turn to you for guidance and support because you alone can lift them up and help them. I thank you that you bring them your healing love to comfort and let them know that they have our compassionate understanding, too, as we feel their pain and spiritual anguish.

Now for the Good News

For eight terrible years I suffered from deep depression brought on by the deaths of my brother and a man I was planning to marry. They died within 11 months of each other. Life for me became intolerable. I wanted to die too. I prayed to die.

During those eight years I suffered panic attacks so that my life was nothing but fear. Fear of living, fear of losing anyone else whom I loved.

89

I knew, though, that if I was to be helped at all it would come from 'up there'! It did, from the day I attended your El Shaddai Healing Mass one year ago. To me it was like a miracle and I do not use that word lightly.

The pain in my heart and memory has gone and a different kind of happiness has come into my life. I know that I will never sink into a void like that again because I have now felt and experienced God's love for me. It is one thing to be taught about God's love, quite another to feel it, and I felt it.

I can say to anyone, whatever your problem, go to a healing Mass, believe in the healing power of our Lord and your problem will be gone and replaced by a love that surpasses all earthly love.

I thank you with all my heart for bringing me closer to God's love. It has changed my life. Now I am no longer afraid.

ANGELA

❦ **LORD**, I have known what it is to find myself lost in the valley of darkness and depression. In those times, you came to me in fleeting moments with the assurance that all would eventually be well. Today may the power of your Spirit be the breath beneath my wings and bear me up so that I may fly like an eagle to a place where I shall find light and peace.

Our granddaughter is on the pill

When my husband and I were baby sitting for my daughter Joan, a single parent, I had to clean out my granddaughter's room. It was like a bombsite. There were condom packets and pills everywhere. Sarah is only 14, and she treats her mother like dirt. It is all so harrowing. What should we do in practical terms?

MABEL

Well, you started anyway by cleaning out Sarah's room. She

will not understand or accept why you did it. She will probably regard you as an interfering old busybody. The state of her room tells you what is going on in her mind and life. It is not so much a cry for help as a statement of fact. I am glad I don't face it. I don't think I would know how to cope!

Don't nag Sarah. Let her be. It is Joan who would seem to be the source of the disorder. She probably allows her daughter to 'treat her like dirt' because this is what she feels she deserves. What kind of life does your daughter lead? Is she happy and fulfilled? What sort of people are her friends? Does she really accept her daughter's attitude and way of life? Is she beaten by it? Has she ever confronted her daughter, and if so what was the outcome? The cause of Sarah's disorder goes back a long way in the family tree. The blame perhaps lies not in her family, but in the sickness of our society.

Don't worry yourselves too much. Worry solves nothing. Try and get closer to Sarah if she will let you. You need to be very sensitive. Don't expect quick results, and be prepared for an emotional bashing. In this situation you and your husband need healing and spiritual strength. I pray for this for you.

❦ HOLY SPIRIT, you hide many things from our knowledge in order to spare us anguish and distress. I pray today for all parents and grandparents who are emotionally hurt by their families, especially in moral issues. Give them your grace to sustain them in their time of sad discovery with its consequent pain. Give them a clearer understanding of the difficulties which our young people face in our free-thinking modern world, which ignores our Christian values. May they retain a loving relationship with their children so that when any future crisis arises, they will be able to assist them by example and gentleness to come to a decision according to your holy will. May they never, however strong the temptation, cut themselves off from the young people of their family but always retain a warm relationship with them just as your Father does with us, despite our sinfulness and pride.

Our son is a Jehovah's Witness

Our only son has joined the Jehovah's Witnesses along with his wife and two young children. He seems very happy and tries to convert us. He is not the only case in our parish. Why is this happening?

BERNARD

Forty years ago if you left the Catholic Church you gave up religion altogether. It is not so today. Some of our best young people in their search for God in their lives have found him in other Churches and groups. God is saying something to us in the present situation and we need to listen to his voice.

Why are young people not finding God in our parish groups?

Because we are too strict? Jehovah's Witnesses make far more demands on their followers than we do. I would not like to live by their rules: I think they are far too strict and unbending. Yet these rules are accepted completely because of what the new religion gives those who join.

What do they receive? Without exception they will tell you that they feel they belong. They are part of a family in which all the members are concerned for one another. They say they have found friends and their new religion is a way of life.

Is my answer in praise of the Jehovah's Witnesses? No, but it is a challenge to us to realise that we Catholics are not seen to be as caring, as friendly, as demanding as Christ our Leader would have us be. Our approach to liturgy must change but this is but the tip of the iceberg which we must recognise as a danger signal if the ship of the Church is not to go on the rocks. Christ is with us. We need to follow him and read the signs of the times.

❦ **HOLY SPIRIT**, I thank you for the gift of my faith in Jesus Christ, my Lord and Saviour, and for the many blessings I have received from you. I thank you for having placed me through no merit of my own, in the holy Catholic Church, which has been for me a very powerful and unique way of living out to the full my Christian life. I thank you that Jesus came into our world as one of us and died for our sake so that in his resurrection we might share in his eternal life. I thank you for all the special people in my life who enabled me to receive your special gift of experiencing a personal God as my Father. I thank you that you are blessing other members of other Churches with the grace of your life and presence. May more people come to know you as I have done through my spiritual brothers and sisters in the Church which is Christ's body.

I'm sixty next birthday

This year – in fact next month – I shall be 60. I'm not going to celebrate my birthday. I'm afraid of growing old and for the first time in my life I'm not going to tell people my age. Am I vain?

NANCY

You are as old or as young as you feel. Age has nothing to do with it. It is all a question of attitude. I never ask people how old they are. Age is only the measure of days you have lived on this earth. What you did with those days and how you feel towards them is the important thing. I know people in their thirties who are mentally older than others twice their age.

Nancy, you have got it wrong. Be yourself. Be what you want to be. Never mind what other people think. You have to love yourself at every stage of your life. You are never too old to be young. Youth is within you in your peace, joy and fulfilment. Live life to the full. Don't waste time thinking of your age. Concentrate on life. It will help you to feel younger than people who are older than you.

✝ LORD, eternal lover of life, help me to savour and enjoy life at every period of my life. May I waste none of its moments and always see them as your gift to me. Life is an adventure with its challenges and rewards when I live it to the full as your Son Jesus Christ would have me do.

When we meet again

I am a retired doctor in my eighty-first year. I have attended a great number of patients in their dying hours, some who died very scared, some in such pain that they were 'happy' to accept death as a merciful relief, and others who died happily in prayer, and often with a smile. The latter category were mostly RCs. I attended four convents in my area, and I found the dear nuns were exemplary at their time of death.

I am most fortunate in having a grand wife, who, like myself, has been a weekly communicant for fifty years. I had two wonderful parents, who reared six boys and two sisters, all excellent Catholics.

When I pass on, will we all meet again and recognise one another? If the answer is positive, then I look forward to my demise most happily.

DR JIM

Jim, you have been very blessed. Your life has been surrounded by all that is best in the Catholic Church. Your parents lived a life of deep faith which was an example to you and your brothers and sisters. Their influence for good passed from them to you in a thousand and one different ways. It did not end with their death. It is part of you still. That is why you want to meet them again, and share with them in heaven just as you did on earth when you grew up together in a truly

Christian family. They are your 'cloud of witnesses' (Hebrews 12:1), encouraging you to live out your life on earth in hope and expectation until you meet again.

Of course you will know and recognise them, but it will be in a new and more beautiful way. There will be an awareness of the great love you have for God and for each other. On earth you sowed the seeds of friendship, and in heaven God will bring them to a full flowering. You are not afraid of death because you see it as the beginning of a new life where age will not matter. The only emotion you will share with your parents and your family is love of God your Father who loved you from the moment you were conceived and born into a loving Christian family.

How you will recognise them I do no know, for we live with the 'God of surprises' but the surprise will be a happy one. We are never separated from the ones we loved but lost awhile. I find Fr Bede Jarrett's prayer very helpful: 'Life is eternal and love is immortal, and death is only an horizon, and an horizon is nothing save the limit of our sight. Lift us, strong Son of God, that we may see further: draw us closer to yourself that we may know ourselves to be nearer to our loved ones who are with you.'

Dr Jim, you have something to look forward to, and you will not be disappointed.

❦ **JESUS**, your risen life is the great hope and anchor of our belief as Christians. I thank you that I believe that I shall meet again in eternal life those who in this mortal life I have loved and lost awhile. In you, there is no death, only a temporary parting from family and friends. You enriched my life through my family and friends. You will bring us all together again in heaven so that we may love you, and each other, in a new and more perfect way.

Why are people so angry?

I am very unhappy and disturbed by the anger in our society. Why are people so lacking in patience and courtesy. It is not the peaceful society I grew up in. What is the cause of it all?

TED

Your world and mine as we knew it is gone for ever. It was not as good or as bad as we like to remember. It was good in parts and, depending on our attitude, we will see it as we choose. I prefer to be positive, I like to look on it as St Paul did: He said 'this may be a wicked world, but our lives should redeem it.' Jesus reminds us that we have to read the signs of the times and adapt to them as God would have us do.

Ted, we need discernment to separate the good things from the bad. In our consumer, computer-controlled society people seem less personal because the pressures on them have increased dramatically. You have only to drive a car to realise how frustrated people feel deep inside!

In their hearts, people want the simple life, but those who control society's thinking have not got the message right. People are angry because they know that they are missing out on the real values in life. Everything they need to give a balance to their lives is being destroyed or belittled. They want someone and some organisation to speak up for the true values which are relevant to every age and every class of society. This is the Church's mission. I blame the media for many of our problems. They have got it wrong. If I am angry with anyone, I am angry with them. The peace Christ offers us is not of this world either in ages past or today. Ted, be at peace within yourself and let the noise of the world fall on deaf ears.

❦ HOLY SPIRIT, I pray today for peace in our world and an end to violence. May there be peace in our homes and hearts so that when we go about our daily work, we may do so in a spirit of peace and harmony. Teach me to realise that I share my world with others, many of whom are less fortunate than I am, and feel resentment at their lot in life. Help me to understand their frustration which often expresses itself in violence and anger. Purify the minds and attitudes of those in leadership positions in our society, especially in the media, so that they present a better, more peaceful view of our world, rather than the violent image on which those troubled in spirit will feed. May the world we live in know Christ's peace without which society loses its direction and ignores our human desire for peace.

Why does my mother suffer?

My mother is the finest, most generous and caring person I know. She has had a hard life raising a large family. She nursed my father with tenderness over a very long, harrowing illness until he died last year. She has just been told by her doctor that she has terminal cancer. We are all heartbroken for her. Why did God allow this to happen to someone so special?

BERNARD

I know to some extent how you feel. I have been down that dark road myself when my mother died. It is impossible to put into words the pain we feel inside when someone whom we love suffers. We would willingly take their place if we could. Of course you are right to ask God, 'Why her Lord? What wrong has she done? Why didn't you spare her this? Don't you really care for someone as special as my mother? Are you oblivious to all the hurt that this illness is causing our family, especially our beloved mother?'

Bernard, you would not be a loving son if you felt otherwise. I would be less than honest if I pretended I had an easy answer to the whole problem of suffering. It is a mystery. The apostles did not understand Jesus when he said he had to suffer. This is not a time for platitudes as you stand helplessly by. Mary stood by the cross and watched her son die. Here is the Pietá – the symbol of compassionate suffering. Bernard, when you can explain Calvary then I shall give you an answer to your question. All I can say now is that its purpose is hidden from our eyes. You will see your mother again in a place where there is no suffering or pain. Your mother will not die for ever. You see, Bernard, we are an Easter people who believe in the resurrection. Without this belief we have no answer to your question.

❧ LORD, make me realise that by simply suffering for Jesus' sake, I can often do more for others than by being active in caring for them. It is hard for me to understand this, so please make me accept that my very helplessness in the presence of suffering makes me aware of how much help you have to offer me and those in pain for whom I care. Suffering works mysteriously in a way which is beyond my powers of reasoning because it creates life and transforms everything it touches when it flows from your cross and from pain endured for our sake. Open my eyes to see beyond the darkness of suffering to the light and dawn of a new life in the resurrection.

My prayers are dry

When I say my prayers I often wonder if there is anyone listening 'out there'. I say my prayers as part of my religious routine, but I don't feel any response. Is this normal?

MARTHA

God is not 'out there'. He is within you, Martha and that is where he wants to be. Prayer has more to do with *listening* to what is inside you, rather than talking to someone about it, even if you think that person is God. Prayer is part of you. It is not always in words, or set forms of prayer. It is being aware of a power within you which is greater than you are yourself. It is being conscious that you are loved more than you love yourself. Prayer is all about love. It is not just our love for God, but his love for us.

When I pray, with or without words, I know God will answer me. He knows better than I do what I need and He will give it to me generously and lovingly. Prayers should never be routine. It is rude to pray like that. It is like reading a newspaper at the dining table when you should be sharing with your friend. If this is not good manners, then rolling off words parrot-fashion to God who wants us to share our lives with him is not.

They say, Martha that the longest journey is from the head to the heart. Try to make this journey today when you pray. Don't say anything until you become aware that God is within you loving you. You will feel a response because you will not only know that God is there. You will experience him. Happy listening.

❦ HOLY SPIRIT, give me an awareness of my Father's loving presence whenever I go through life feeling so alone that even my prayers are as dry and parched as an endless barren desert. May I find an oasis in your presence so that I do not feel the need to use words because you are already there with and for me. Give me the assurance to listen, the serenity to be still and the faith to believe that all I am and feel in my barreness is a prayer, because, in lonely quiet places, I am more prepared to listen to my Father who loves and cares for me than to use words which do not express my dearest inner feelings.

Now for the Good News

I am 18 years old and this month I begin my new life as a university student. I never thought I would reach this stage because until recently my life has been filled with uncertainty, self-doubt and fear about the future. God changed all that for me over the past two years. I was once filled with so much anxiety that I could not relate to anyone, not even my parents, and my studies were drastically affected. When I first came to an El Shaddai service two years ago I was like a frightened rabbit. I could not bear anyone to come near me to pray for my healing. I didn't know what healing was all about anyway. Then you and your team prayed over me, and I knew God was changing me inside. I felt as if I was coming out of a dark tunnel, not into a blinding light, but a warm glow which assured me I had nothing or no one to fear.

Since then the progress that has taken place in my life is brilliant. I prayed for those who hurt me. When I forgave them from my heart, I felt a great burden lift from me. If people don't think that you are very hurt when you are young they are mistaken. I know now in my heart that God loves me and wants me to be myself. I was told this in my religious education classes, but this time it was different. I experienced God's love within me. Today I face the challenge of university with a certain amount of uncertainty, but I shall win through because I think I know who I am and who God is. This is what is really worth knowing.

SUSAN

❦ **LORD JESUS CHRIST**, you told us not to worry or be anxious. You know that each day has enough troubles of its own and we are not to burden ourselves with memories of yesterday's problems, or be worried about tomorrow's possible difficulties. Give me then a mind at rest knowing that my Father is sensitive to all my needs for which he will provide. Place in my mind the conviction that I do not face any obstacle that may come my way alone because you are with me to lighten the burden and give strength to my spirit. Tomorrow will look after itself, and yesterday is in your merciful care because you have already taken it to yourself. So having nothing to fear, I shall with your help live this day, and all the days of my life, in your peace.

I am a compulsive gambler

I am a compulsive gambler. I know that it is ruining, not only my own life, but that of my wife and children as well. I love them, but I just cannot stop, even to the extent that my debts may cause us to sell our home. I turn to you in desperation. Please help me.

NICK

Most of us like a flutter on a big sporting event like the Derby, or a weekly ticket in the National Lottery. The danger is that we might not know when to stop. Like the alcoholic with drink, so you have allowed gambling to so bewitch you that it has taken over your life. You love your wife and children, but you have to face the fact that gambling has taken priority over everything else, including them. If you want to show your love for them in a practical way then you have to make the sacrifice of deciding never to gamble again for the rest of your life. The first bet is like the little drink now and again which the alcoholic wrongly thinks cannot do him much harm.

Nick, you have an emotional disease which may prove terminal not only for your own happiness in life, but also for your wife and family. We have alcoholics and gamblers at our El Shaddai healing services; they are still addicted, but non-practising. Bill is someone like you. At our healing meetings he sometimes leads us in the song, 'One day at a time, sweet Jesus'. He knows that he has to face his addiction every morning of his life. He has not won yet – no gambler ever does – Nick, but he is winning. I want you to be like that, so please keep in touch. I want to help you to help yourself.

101

✝ **LORD JESUS,** in times of trial and temptation may I remain close to you so that I am aware that I do not stand alone. Be my friend, my strength and my encourager as once more I feel I cannot withstand the impulse to indulge my weakness. Teach me not to fear the darkness as long as I look towards you who are my light and my hope. It is in times of darkness and crisis especially that I become more aware of your inspiring light, leading me to believe that with your help, I shall overcome. May the experiences I have had in my life of your healing presence encourage me to make others aware of your love and power to help all those who in time of temptation call on your holy name.

A false notion of God

I was reared on the idea of a just God who would punish us for any wrong we did. Fifty years on I am unable to break free from the spectre of an angry God. I try to love him, but I can't because his 'justice' gets in the way. What should I do?

JANET

You are a victim of a false notion of God: a God who watches over us with a stern critical eye, and when we do wrong says, 'You'll pay for that'. He is a judge whose justice is para-mount. It blots out his love for us as Father. This love is reserved for the good and holy. He is a selective God who must be slavishly obeyed. If we die in sin then we will fall into his hands and he will punish us with eternal fire and torture greater than any we can imagine. His punishment chills the heart and we try to keep out of sin so that we will make it to heaven.

If this is your God, he is not mine. You have been brought up on this carricature of God. I have heard it preached and taught myself but I rejected it long ago. It is false and untrue to the Gospel of Jesus Christ. He told us to look on God as our Father. Jesus identified with us and called us friends. The prayer he gave us is the Our Father. If we fail to acknowledge God as someone who never stops loving us then we are not Christians. The message of Jesus will not get through to us and so far as we are concerned he might as well not have come on earth.

Janet, there are far too many people like you whose minds and hearts have been warped by false teaching. I'm afraid your healing will take a long time. You need help. May I suggest that our El Shaddai tape *The Healing of Fear and False Guilt* and my book *Do Not Be Afraid* will help you to erase the false teaching you received. Those who teach and preach fear are really projecting their own fears. They too need healing and we pray for them. God wants to be loved not feared. He is a loving, caring, understanding Father.

❦ GOD OUR FATHER, sometimes I have found it difficult to come to you because I have been given false notions about you. I have been wrongly taught that you were such a severe judge that you punished me for anything I did wrong. I looked on you as a tyrant over my life that to disobey you meant eternal punishment and the fires of hell. I come to you today and ask you to forgive my ignorance which blighted so many years of my life. Teach me to love you more from this day onwards so that my fear may disappear and the rest of my life may be lived in love and peace with you.

I'm not happy at work

I work to keep a roof over my family's head. I don't enjoy what I do, and I'm making my wife and family miserable. I feel so guilty about it. Any suggestions?

BILL

We live in a society which increasingly sees workers as cogs in

103

a machine. The workplace has become a treadmill in which survival is the name of the game. The microchip has shrunk men and women to things of very little value. Is it any wonder that there is so much frustration, unhappiness and misery among people such as yourself? We are all feeling the strain and tension in a depersonalised society.

Whenever I conduct a healing service I am conscious of the pain in the people who come looking, like you, Bill, for an answer to this problem. I'm sure God did not mean us to live like this but we all feel so powerless to change the monstrous system.

Bill, try to make the best of your situation. Share as openly as you can with your wife and family. They are your biggest asset. Try, however, not to overburden yourself or your family with your worries. They have their problems, too. Your home is your oasis in a desert, the eye of the storm where you can be still and happy. If you keep your family values right you will not go far wrong. This after all is what will bring you happiness and peace.

❦ HEAVENLY FATHER, you have designed our world so that through our labour we co-operate with you in producing those goods necessary for life. It is your plan that we should all be engaged in work which enhances rather than hinders our human dignity. Because greed and lack of appreciation of the value of the human person, many of us are frustrated and unhappy and are being destroyed as persons by the way we are treated as unimportant components in an uncaring system. Give me the courage to speak up for the true value of human labour, and may I be sensitive to the worries and hopes of those who share with me in my place of employment.

I never showed love to my father

My father was a strict disciplinarian. Although he was a good man, he never showed his family that he loved them. I obeyed and respected him, but I never told him I loved him.

He died without knowing my need to love and be loved by him. I agonise now years later over my failure to make personal contact. What should I do?

SARAH

Your father probably acted the way he did because this was the way he was treated himself. You only show love when you have experienced it. He was damaged himself and in turn passed on the hurt to those who were nearest and dearest to him. There are so many crippled parents who don't know how to treat their children. They are either too strict or over-indulgent. Both attitudes are equally damaging.

Sarah, it is understandable but unproductive to feel guilty. The past is dead and you cannot bring it back. Your father and you missed out on something precious. The best way to show your love for him now is not to let the past cloud your present life and happiness. By all means feel sorry for him and remember his good points. Remember that he was the product of his age and training. You are much freer, thank God. If you have a family then learn from past mistakes. When you meet your father again in heaven there will be no need to say 'sorry'. You will both experience love in a new and beautiful way. The world of the past will be gone. The new one will be God's way of showing he loves you both.

❦ FATHER from whom all fatherhood comes, grant me your peace and forgiveness for my lack of love for my father during his earthly life. May I remember all the good times I shared with him so that I may understand him better. Excuse my not telling him I loved him and my lack of sympathy in understanding the lack of love in our family during the years of his life. May I be consoled with the thought that when we meet in heaven, we will both experience love for each other in a new and beautiful way.

My daughter's registry office wedding

My daughter has not been to church since she left school. She wants to be married in a registry office because she says it would be hypocritical to marry in church. Her father and I are deeply hurt. What shall we do on the wedding day? Do we boycott it completely because we do not want to condone what she is doing? Your advice please.

DOROTHY

You are in a dilemma. You love your daughter and because of what your religion means to you, you want to see her married in church. Because you love her, you must not lose contact with your daughter. If you do then everything is lost. I presume you have spoken gently with her and so she knows how you feel. She is right about not wanting to be a hypocrite. Too many use the church as a social occasion for a 'posh' wedding. Tell her she may be 'lapsed' now, but that it is never too late to return.

Speak to her and her fiancé, Dorothy, together. Listen to their reasons with openness and understanding. Try to see things from their point of view. Pray about it first and God will give you the right words and attitude. If they still insist on a registry office wedding you will have made your point about your conscience. I would suggest that you do not go to the registry office, but attend the wedding reception. I advise this because you must leave bridges for your daughter to cross. In the future, if grandchildren come along, you will be there to encourage their parents to have them baptised.

You are not condoning the way they choose to be married. You are showing your mother's love for your daughter. Take the long term view. See beyond the wedding to the future.

God knows how you feel. Surely this is the most important thing. I pray and hope that all will be well.

☙ **HOLY SPIRIT**, fill my mind and heart with love for all my family. May my love for them flow over to those whom they love. Let no word or action of mine ever cause disharmony which would break my family relationships. I thank you for giving me a deep appreciation of my faith and protecting me in those situations when it was at risk. Be with all parents today when family values are under attack, and when their children no longer follow their Christian calling. Console and strengthen them so that their pain and disappointment may be lightened by the hope that all will come well in the future because you watch over and protect them with your unceasing love.

Now for the Good News . . .

I have wanted to write to you for a long time to let you know of our good news. My daughter, Jennie, who could not talk has started to do so. She says quite a few odd words, and even a few sentences. She loves Our Lady, whom she calls 'My Lady', very much.

The second piece of good news is that the last two scans I have had for cancer have been clear. I am so grateful to you and to everyone for all their kindness and prayers over the past five years. You, and the El Shaddai team, helped me when my father died. I had a lot of grief and pain inside which I could not let go until you prayed over me five years ago. It was the first time I was able to cry after my father's death. It was like a weight had been lifted from my shoulders.

Over the past ten years my sister, my sister-in-law, my baby boy, my father and my two granddads have all died. During this time my faith has just got stronger and stronger. I know that Jesus is always with me, and there is nothing in life that I have to go through alone.

In the next few weeks I shall be starting instructions to join the Catholic faith. I have thought about it for a long time, but I now know the time is right. What my husband and I have been through is nothing compared to what other people suffer in their lives. I know I wouldn't be where I am today if it was not for Our Lord, and all the help he has given me through yourself. Thank you and God bless you.

MELANIE

❦ HOLY SPIRIT, you are with me always, renewing and healing me. There are times when there is such tragedy all around me that I feel unable to cope with life and dread the next disaster which will befall me. It is on these occasions that you calm the storm, soothe my frayed and anxious thoughts, and bring me a peace beyond all describing which fills me with confidence and hope so that I can face my world with courage and resolve. I know that all will be well because you are with and within me. All around me in the midst of sadness and pain, I see your healing power at work in the most disastrous circumstances rebuilding your people, changing situations and manifesting your love in a way which helps to deepen my faith, renew my hope and give me a love of you which is my peace and inspiration.

I just cannot pray

I do not know how to pray. I envy people who can say the Rosary. After the first decade, I get distracted. I love God and I want to pray to him. Please help me.

PETER

No one but God's Spirit can teach you how to pray. He will show you which way is best for you. He is showing you now.

Prayer should flow from within you. It cannot be forced. Never mind how others pray. We are all unique. You pray the way the Spirit guides you. All I can do is offer suggestions.

The only way to learn to pray is to pray. If you really want to pray well then pray often. Start off with a short morning prayer offering your day to God. Long prayers are not for you at the present moment. Be aware during the day of God's presence and his love for you. Do the same at night time. Just a few short prayers that you know already and which suit your temperament. Soon you will grow in prayer.

I have made a tape *Praying for Healing* which I hope will help you. It explains in very simple language how prayer heals us and brings us inner peace by making us aware that God loves us as a Father. Hundreds of people have written to say how much it has helped them. I hope it will help you, too.

❦ **SPIRIT** of the living God, teach me how to pray. Make my spirit to rest in you, my heart to love you, my mind to be filled with thoughts of you and my whole being to be open to the promptings of your Spirit. Help me to believe that God my Father never fails both to hear and to answer every prayer that is sincere, since He hears not so much the voice as the heart. May I open my heart to him so that he may fill it with his love and peace.

A family at war

My family is forever feuding. We all bear grudges against each other. It has crippled me emotionally all through my life. What can I do to bring about reconciliation between my brothers and sisters?

MARGARET

A family at war is a very wounding conflict. It is a series of never-ending battles in which no one wins and everyone is

109

damaged. It is one of the most difficult situations to resolve, and invariably the peacemaker is rounded on by all sides.

You probably know that already, Margaret, from any attempts you may have made at reconciliation. Yet you know that you must keep on trying. In situations like yours, I am encouraged by the words of St Paul: Christ is the peace between us, and has made the two into one, and broken down the barrier which used to keep us apart (Ephesians 2:14). Family rifts are soul-destroying and people often take their hatred and bitterness to the grave. You must safeguard your own inner peace. Do not let any member of your family take it from you.

Prayer is the one vital factor which will bond the family together where there is a lot of healing to be done. I know this from my own time working for peace in Northern Ireland in the late 1970s. Don't take sides or you will be lost in the conflict. If and when an opportunity presents itself, speak to an individual brother or sister in a gentle, non-accusing way. These opportunities, such as personal crises, will be a gift from God for you to pour in your healing ointment. You will need the Holy Spirit, but tread carefully. You are entering an emotional minefield. May God go with you.

❦ FATHER, thank you for having created us and given us to each other in the human family. Thank you for being with us in all our joys and sorrows, for your comfort in our sadness, your companionship in our loneliness. Thank you for family, for friends and for your loving presence among us. Bring peace to all those who suffer discord in their families, and grant that they be reconciled to each other so that your peace may descend on them and remain always with them. Grant that they will grow together as a loving family who share their lives in love and harmony.

Now for the Good News

I want to tell you how God taught me to love myself.

I was very happily married, pretty successful in business and had a large circle of friends. Then suddenly the company for which I worked went bankrupt. However hard I tried I could not find suitable alternative employment. I soon lost confidence in myself, and I was unable to maintain my previous standard of living. My 'friends' gradually melted away out of my life. My wife, Patricia, stood by me but I knew that I was disintegrating as a person. I saw no hope for the future and the fear of what might happen to our family disturbed my sleeping and waking hours. In fact, I just could not sleep. I began to hate myself for the trouble I had brought on those I loved. I saw no purpose in life. I lost my peace of mind. I felt, too, that I was losing my faith in God.

Then one day I went to a healing service in which the whole message was that God loved us as only a true Father could. No matter what happened to us or what difficulties we were in, God's love for us was constant. He would never fail to give us love and courage to live to the full especially in the bad times when nothing seems to go right for us and we look at the future in gloom and despair. The service changed my life. My relationship with Patricia and the children has deepened and we are a happier family now than we have ever been. I know God is my loving Father, not only in my mind but also in my heart. Fear does not rule my life and I feel as free as the birds in the air because I know I have a reason for loving myself. My greatest wealth is to know and love myself as a person whom God loves.

*

I wrote this letter over six weeks ago but never posted it. Here is more good news. Last week I was called for an interview for a senior post in a firm similar to the one I had to leave. I was successful. It is everything in business I could have wanted but now I know where my priorities lie. In my time of crisis what I lost I found and by this I mean God's love for me which taught me to value myself, my wife and children and the right things in life.

JOHN

❦ **SPIRIT OF TRUTH**, I praise you that you have taught me to value the correct things in life. My love for you is the one constant value in my life which never changes. In all the difficulties which came my way, I found you there as my hope and support. Without you I know that many times I would have failed and not been able to face my problems with courage and conviction. Your love has driven fear out of my life, and brought me a sense of belonging and inner security which is my most treasured possession. I pray for all those who feel they cannot cope with life. May they turn to you in their perplexity, and discover your love for them which gives them the strength and understanding they need to believe in themselves and resolve the problems which cause them anxiety.

I have been made redundant

I am only 35, and I have been redundant for 18 months. I just cannot find employment however hard I try. I have lost all my self confidence. I am increasingly irritable with my wife and children, and the future is bleak. Where is God in all this?

PAUL

He is there, but you cannot see him because the clouds of doubt and despair are hiding him from your vision. Paul, I grieve for you. It is all very well for me to say that because I have never heard of a priest being made redundant. There

112

are too few of us to go round! It is precious little consolation for you to know that redundancy is affecting thousands of people who thought their jobs were secure. They have mortgages to meet and other financial worries which redundancy brings. On top of all that there is the destructive clawing feeling that nobody want your skills and talents. You are tempted to feel worthless in your own eyes. This is probably why you are irritable with your wife and children. You feel you are letting them down.

Paul, you cannot help what happened. You need healing but so does our industrial mentality. Society has denied you your right to work for a living for yourself and those you love. Don't worry if you feel angry and frustrated. It is good to let off steam, but not too much! I am not going to give you pious platitudes which would serve only to make you feel more angry and frustrated. I pray you will find employment soon. God is there for you. Remember, his son told the story of the labourer being called into the vineyard to work at the eleventh hour (Matthew 20:6). Please God your time will come soon.

✿ HEAVENLY FATHER, who wills that every individual should belong to the human community, look with compassion on all those who have been made redundant in their place of employment. Take from them the feeling of resentment, bitterness and rejection, and may they soon find a new fulfilling avenue for their skills. May they take strength and hope from the gospel story told by Jesus of those who were called to labour in the vineyard at the eleventh hour.

My husband is a bachelor

My husband, David, does his own thing. Soon after we were married he went out to the pub with his friends every night. He lives a bachelor life. I am not possessive and I want him to have time and space for himself, but what about me? Our marriage is practically dead. What should I do about it?

There are many married 'bachelors' and 'spinsters'. They do not realise that marriage is a sharing with another person and involves them in changing their way of life. Our suitability for marriage is shown in our awareness that we need a partner in order to be more fulfilled as a person. Marriage is a personal relationship which changes us. If it does not, then we are not really married in the sense that we are not changed by our relationship.

Norah, you have got a problem. There are many ways of handling it. The one thing you must not do is to even the score and go off with your friends every evenings. You would soon be strangers living in the same house, although it looks as if you are nearly that way already. Try and get David to sit down and talk with you about the things you could and should share together. Ask him why he got married in the first place. Tell him gently, patiently, and as lovingly as you can what you want your marriage to be. Ask him how he sees it.

This is not going to be an easy affair for either of you. Unless you talk now in order to kindle any hope that might be left, then in a short time it may be too late. I pray for you both. We all have to share in life whether married or otherwise. You and David need to have a good look at your relationship. He can have his night out with the 'boys' but only after you both have shared deeply as two people who so loved each other that you chose to get married.

❦ **LORD JESUS CHRIST**, you shared your life completely, not only with your mother and your followers, but also with all those who came to you for help and healing. You never refused your friendship to anyone. I know that if I am to be a

114

Christian, I must be ready to offer my friendship to those whom I encounter in my pilgrimage through life. I thank you for your example in which you showed that friendship is a giving of oneself to another. I thank you for all those who by their friendship have nurtured my life and helped me to grow as a person. I pray especially for married couples who suffer because they are deprived of a true and complete sharing of their partners. May their relationship blossom so that they know the value of sharing in marriage without which no union can grow.

My trouble with step-children

My husband George lost his first wife four years ago, and two years later married me. We are the same age group, have so much in common and are very happy together. His grown-up family, however, resents me and they make life extremely difficult for their father. I've tried everything but can't break the barriers down.

CLARE

Perhaps you are trying too hard. Let the family be. They perhaps regard their father as their exclusive property. To them you are an outsider. You are not part of the family. They look upon George as their father and not as a person who needs the love and companionship of a partner with whom he can share.

It is difficult to advise you, Clare, because I do not know all the circumstances behind their attitude. You and George must stand firmly together in order to protect your love for each other. The family must not be allowed to threaten that. In some ways, George's marriage to you is an acknowledgment that he needs the fulfilment of companionship which he experienced in his first marriage. His family obviously do not see this and are unwilling to adapt to the new situation.

115

Don't force them, or bend over backwards to please them. They have to make part of the journey towards you if peace, love and reconciliation are to be achieved. Never discuss them negatively. Your love for George is the key which will help to unlock the door to his family's minds and hearts. It may well be a long healing process. Don't be impatient or jealous. George needs you. This is why he married you. Concentrate on that and hopefully the rest will fall into place.

✣ **LORD JESUS**, you blessed the human family by spending most of your life with your mother, Mary, and Joseph at your home in Nazareth. There you grew to maturity and by your obedient loving presence, you raised the dignity of the family to a pinnacle in which the human race was to find its ideal. Today, we pray for all families, especially where there is discord between the children and step-parents. Lord, I pray that all those suffering from such a stress will open their hearts to the new situation, and not exclude anyone from a loving relationship. May their homes be blessed with your presence so that parents and children may grow together in love and peace and a true appreciation of one another's value.

Shall I postpone my wedding?

My wedding is arranged for next spring, but I'm worried about my fiancé's attitude. He refuses to talk seriously about our future together. He seems to drift along and I can't seem to get him to discuss and share deeply. We are both in our early twenties, and I wonder if we should wait a little longer.

JANE

Yes. You should wait a little longer! Marriage is the most serious step you will both take together. If you cannot discuss things seriously now then you will not be prepared later for

116

situations in your marriage when they arise. You should not enter marriage blindly. This is a recipe for disaster and divorce. Are you pushing your views too much? Is your fiancé really ready for marriage? Are you? You are both young, so unless you can share together at a deep level now then at least postpone the wedding. You have everything to gain and nothing to lose by doing this. From my own experience as a priest the situation you describe has been all too common and is a source of great pain to those involved.

Never mind what your families and friends think. It is your life and happiness, not theirs, which is at stake. Find a counsellor or person whose opinion you trust and seek their advice. You are showing your love for your fiancé by wanting what is best for you both when you share your life together. If you cannot have a closer mutual understanding of your vision of married life then maybe it is better to part now rather than later. You have a hard decision to make but if you love each other then you will come closer together. Be patient. True love will find a way.

❦ **FATHER**, we pray for all those contemplating marriage that they do so with an awareness of their responsibility to make all the emotional and spiritual preparations necessary for such an important decision. May your Spirit help them to discern their needs, and may your Son, Jesus, be with them in their hearts on their wedding day.

Now for the Good News

Some weeks ago a woman called Madge wrote to you. She was afraid of going blind. There must be many people like her. I know, because I was one of them. Let me tell you my story.

Sixteen years ago, I had glaucoma in both eyes for which there was no cure. At best it could be controlled with eye drops. I was admitted to hospital immediately for observation. It was discovered that the glaucoma was so advanced in my left eye that I could lose my sight from it at any time. It was operated on seven years ago, and the right eye on the following year. Both operations were successful. Last year I had a cataract removed from the right eye. I am now 82 years old and have always prayed with confidence to God that I would have reasonable sight till the end of my days. I know that God answers prayers because he certainly answered mine. I have been a widow for 21 years and I have no family. We need faith if we really want to trust that God will look after us. Thank you, Father Michael, for the understanding way you answer people's problems and fears. We all need to help each other. This is the secret of healing.

By the way, I am now able to cross the road myself and even thread a needle! So my prayers are answered. I can appreciate all the beautiful colours of the flowers again. I think God is wonderful. My eyesight is his gift to me.

KATE

❦ **LORD JESUS**, just as you gave sight to the blind, renew in me my life of faith. Lend me your vision so that I may see again the beauty of your life, and know the thrill of your message, which makes me see beyond the limited horizon I would have if I were left to my own resources. I praise you for the many people whose lives you have changed and renewed once they became aware of your loving presence. They saw again in faith because you touched them gently, and once they found you, they wanted to know you more, and never leave your presence. Bless today all who are blind, not only to physical sight, but to a personal awareness of you and the healing you bring. Open their eyes, Lord, so that they may see the beauty of your life and world.

I am not at peace

I am not at peace with myself and never have been. Hardly a day goes by but something crops up which disturbs me, and throws me off balance. What do you mean by peace and how do I get it?

TOM

If we want to be really happy, then we need to be at peace with ourselves, and our lifestyle. Peace and happiness are two sides of the same coin. Our Christian faith teaches us how to be happy and joyful. Jesus said that he came so that we might share his joy and peace (John 15:11.)

Tom, you need to love yourself in a very open fulfilling way. Take each day as a blessing from God, each person you meet is someone who wants to be your friend.

Don't see people as enemies or a threat if you want to be at peace in your mind and heart. If you cannot be at peace with some people, then avoid them and find others with whom you can relate as a friend. If you can't find anyone then you are really in trouble and you should take a closer look inside yourself. Peace after all begins inside us.

❦ **LORD JESUS**, a peace which the world cannot give is your gift to your followers. Fill my mind and heart with your peace so that I may look at the world through your eyes, and know that your precious gift keeps me serene amid all the trials and tribulations which each day brings. Teach me to discern the peace I should seek, the peace I should keep, and the peace I should share. Peace means loving myself so that I am at peace in every situation in which I find myself. As I journey through life, may I see everyone as a possible friend, and not a potential enemy. As your peace comes to me, like gentle rain or sunshine, so may my peace flow out to others and nourish them so that they, too, grow as persons through your gift of peace.

Can't cope with our children

Our teenage children are playing us up. They stay out some nights and never tell us where they have been except to say that it was with friends. We don't know how to cope.

ALFRED

What parent does? There is no hard and fast rule on how to treat your children because children differ not only in themselves but also from their parents. They belong to a different generation with a different culture and set of values. We have to get behind the appearances to attempt to discover what they are really thinking. I don't think they often know themselves. Life is a puzzle at that age.

Young people need more space than adults. They are in a learning situation with new experiences to which they have to make the form of response they think is right for them. They can't be told what to do without discussion so don't try. Above all, don't be too negative and prohibitive in your approach. Remember your own youth and the mistakes you made. Did you ever go through a period when you resented your parents' interference? Don't think you never caused them worry or anxiety. Young people respond to challenge, so why not try to be in there with them, encouraging them in all their efforts to come to terms with life.

Open your home to their friends. Encourage them to bring them home. After all, you surely have *your* friends to visit. I'm not being soft. The best way to safeguard your children is to love and tell them how special they are to you. Worrying about them will not change them; love will.

❦ LORD JESUS, you said suffer little children to come unto you for of such was the kingdom of heaven. You experienced the unique relationship between a parent and child in your own life. Once, when you went missing, your mother sought you, worrying until she found you in the temple three days afterwards. You understand that parents do not always know how to cope with their children when they are presented with an unusual situation. They need our prayerful support. We pray for all parents and children everywhere that they may develop a greater understanding of their respective roles through love, tolerance and patience. May they all grow in wisdom together before God their Father as they imitate the example you set in your family life at Nazareth.

I cannot love myself

I just cannot love myself. At home and in church I had it drilled into me that I was unworthy. They did a good job on me because now I cannot see anything really lovable in myself. Please help me.

AMY

You are in a really bad way if you don't love yourself, because it means you cannot love anyone. Jesus taught us that we were to love our neighbour as we love ourselves (Matthew 2:37–39). If you don't love yourself then you can't love anyone. You are living in isolation starved of love and friendship.

God loves you whether you love yourself or not. No matter what you have done with your life God still loves you because he is your father. His love is not conditional. He doesn't love you because you are good. He loves you because he made you. You are his child. No one is worthy of his love, no one deserves it but if those who told you that you were unworthy did not also stress that you are lovable in yourself because God loves you then they have damaged you emotionally and spiritually. They ignored the Christian gospel of love. Amy, love yourself from now on. Make up for lost time. As the song goes, 'love changes everything'. Let it change you.

❦ **ALMIGHTY FATHER**, you created me because you loved me. You meant me to be myself, and to grow in freedom and true love of the person I am as I reach out in hope to the person I want to become. Each day I know that if I am true to myself I shall grow as a person. I also know that if I do not love myself, I cannot love anyone, especially you whom I have never seen. Help me, Lord, to let your love so flow through me that I may love myself as you have loved me even before the world began.

I really hate someone

There is someone at work whom I hate. I have to be nice to him but deep inside I plot all sorts of revenge against him. These thoughts dominate my life and ruin any happiness I might have. What is your advice?

PETER

Hatred is a very insidious emotion. It feeds on jealousy, envy, greed and other evil ingredients. It creeps into every aspect of our lives until it takes us over completely. Thoughts of hatred paralyse us. We lie awake at night plotting our revenge while our 'victim' is sleeping peacefully in his bed. At its lowest level, Peter, don't give your 'enemy' the satisfaction of knowing that he disturbs your peace.

You may be angry with him and perhaps justifiably so, but there is a world of difference between anger and hatred. When your thoughts move from anger to hatred then you have strayed on to very dangerous ground. Jesus was angry with the Pharisees but he didn't hate them. There are many Pharisees around in every organisation. There always have been and always will be. They are the thorns which mask the rose.

So, Peter, be angry with your 'enemy'. When you have got it off your chest, let it be. No one is important enough in our

122

lives to deserve our hatred. Walk away from them in your mind and concentrate on something and someone different. In this way you free yourself from your enemy. Jesus said, 'Love your enemy.' It is not easy, but it is better than hating. Peace be with you.

❦ **LORD JESUS**, you said I was to love my enemies. I have always found this difficult especially when they treat me unjustly. I ask you, Lord, to put your mind and heart within me to learn to forgive them even though it is at present not possible for me to forget. I still bear the scars of what has happened in my spirit and emotions. May I be at peace in my mind and not fill it with thoughts of revenge or getting even. Be with me, Lord, this day as I think of you and how you suffered and forgave your enemies. Fill me with your peace so that there is no room in me for anything to disturb your presence and peace.

I am full of fear

I live in fear. It is the most destructive element in my life. I'm afraid of everything and everybody. Even though I go to daily Mass I still look on God as someone to be feared. Is there any hope for me?

DERMOT

Fear can be a very helpful emotion but only as long as we control it rather than letting it control us. We should be afraid of anything which destroys our inner peace or diminishes us as a person. The right kind of fear protects us from harm. For instance, I would be afraid to jump out of a plane wearing a parachute because I don't know how to use it. It would be a foolish thing to do and so my fear tells me not to try. In that way fear is good.

The great enemy of the wrong kind of fear is faith. You

need to believe that God loves you, otherwise why go to daily Mass? If you go because you fear God then you have got yourself into a terrible mess, and your very going to Mass may only serve to increase your fear. You also need faith in yourself. You must love yourself, and see yourself as lovable. Never mind what other people think or say. The wrong kind of fear tells you that you are proud. The right kind that you have discovered the truth of Christ's message. In love there can be no fear (1 John 4:16–18).

❦ **FATHER**, fear is the enemy of my personal freedom and growth in inner peace. Fearful people go through life growing old but never growing up. I am afraid, Father, of being afraid because it diminishes and destroys my love for you and myself. Send your love into my heart because only your perfect love can cast out my fear. May I see fear as my enemy and with your help may I confront all my hidden fears.

Now for the Good News

My healing started over two years ago at an El Shaddai service at Southwark Cathedral. I was suffering then from an aneurysm of the aorta. The physical problems had started about six months earlier. By Easter I was so ill that my wife, Christine, doubted whether I would survive. I had dreadful pains in my hips and legs. During a scan for kidney stones, the doctor found that my aorta was about 4.7cm – it should be about 2.5cm. After further tests, surgery was advised. This is a major operation. The section of the aorta with the bulge is removed and replaced with an artificial section. There is significant risk in such an operation and it involves a stay of about ten days in hospital, including thirty-six hours in intensive care.

After the Southwark Cathedral service, when I went into hospital, Christine asked the house surgeon if he could do another scan because I felt so much better. He spent the next ten minutes arguing that there was no way an aneurysm could ever get smaller. When I went for surgery my wife's prayer was, 'Lord, you can do a miracle even on the operating table.' When the surgeon cut me open, he found he could not operate because the aorta was inflamed. I realised something odd had happened when I came round in the ward and not in intensive care! The medics were so embarrassed about it all that the surgeon would not talk to Christine after the operation.

I was sent home after three days. Since then I have regained my strength. I no longer have pains in my legs and hips. According to a scan done by a specialist in another hospital, the diameter of my aorta is now about 3.2cm which is well within safe limits. All I have left is a 12 inch scar to remind me that miracles happen when we trust in God.

GRAHAM

❦ **HOLY SPIRIT**, the wonders of your healing are beyond words. They fail to express the many ways in which you reveal your power and teach us to hope again when everything is filled with darkness and despair. I know you have been present to me on so many occasions in my life that now I expect to see your power at work always in my life and that of others. I am no longer surprised at any outcome because you are the God of surprises whose nature it is to heal and make whole our damaged world and people. May all those who have felt your presence and received your gifts, witness to your power so that the world, and all members of Christian Churches, may learn to believe.

God never answers my prayers

I do not say my prayers out of my love for God but rather because of a sense of duty. Does he really care for me? If so, why doesn't he answer my prayers? He never gives me what I ask for, so either he doesn't love me or I'm praying the wrong way. What do you think?

NORAH

Prayer is a very strange thing. It is not a matter of saying a lot of words. Rather prayer is all about listening in love to a God whom we cannot see but yet who lives within us. Prayer is not a journey outside ourselves. It is a discovery within ourselves of the abiding presence of God.

Norah, I presume you are asking God for what you *want* rather than what you *need*. The only way you will come to know the difference is when you listen. Only then will you begin to see your life as it really is, not as you imagine it to be. You know your wants. God would like you to know your needs. When you discover what these are then you can begin to pray. All your prayers will be answered. You will be of one mind with God. He will meet your needs because at last you will be really praying.

❦ JESUS, you told us that whatever we asked of the Father in your name, he would give it to us. Send your Spirit into my life so that I might learn how to pray. May I ask for those things I need rather than what I think I want because you know my needs better than I know them myself. May my every thought and word in prayer flow from my love of the Father who knows and listens to what I say even before the words are on my lips. May I listen to the promptings of your Holy Spirit as I become more aware that what he says to me is more important than anything I could say to him.

I'm a worrier

I am a born worrier. I can't enjoy life because worry takes over everything. I worry about my health, my job, my future and my family. You name it, I worry about it. How do I get myself out of this?

DAVID

Worry solves nothing. It always presents questions but never answers. It creates doubt not certainty. It presents you with alternative solutions of which one is as bad as the other. Worry prevents you from doing things because you are not sure of the consequences of your actions.

Jesus was a 'yes' person. He knew where he was going and why. He was about his father's business and told his followers time and again that once they put their hands to the plough they had to carry on with what they were doing and not turn back. 'Can any of you for all his worrying', he said, 'add a single day to your span of life.' So do not worry about tomorrow: tomorrow will take care of itself. Each day has enough trouble of its own' (Matthew 6:27, 34).

Worry, in fact, shortens life. David, worrying about tomorrow prevents you from living for today and so you cannot cope with today's problems never mind about tomorrow's. You build up a backlog of problems so that your life is crammed full of things that should be done but you never get round to doing because you are worried about something else which in fact might never happen.

David, you were meant to enjoy life. It comes one day at a time. Live it to the full so you will have no room for worry. This is the Christian secret of life and happiness.

❦ **LORD JESUS**, you entrusted your whole life to your heavenly Father. You never worried about the final outcome of any event, even your crucifixion, because you saw worry as a lack of confidence in your Father's willingness and ability to help you. In your many miracles you called on your Father to witness to his love for you. He never failed to respond. In every situation in which I find myself, may I always seek my Father's kingdom first, knowing that everything I need will be given to me as well. For you, Lord, worry divides and distracts a person from the main thing in life which is to give the Father all honour and glory by our trust in him. May I live each day to the full and let tomorrow look after itself because my Father will be with me tomorrow as surely as he is with me today.

I just cannot forgive

You are always writing about forgiveness. I just cannot forgive my father. He was cruel to us and violent to my mother. Even though he died long ago, the memory of him still fills me with bitterness. I need help.

ELIZABETH

The scars of past hurts will always remain. Even when the wounds are healed the after-effects are still there. You are a victim of someone from whom you would have expected to receive love and kindness, yet the memories of his cruelty are uppermost in your mind and heart. There is no room left for feelings of forgiveness. It is always more difficult to forgive parents than anyone else because we have such high expectations of them. When they fail it is doubly hurtful.

The best advice I can give you is not to pretend that it never happened, or to feel guilty because you still feel angry and bitter towards your father. What he did is still haunting you by the memory of what happened. Ask the Lord to ease the pain and gradually to let the painful memories recede into the background. Your father probably had a violent family background when he was young.

Elizabeth, let the violence stop here. The healing of hurtful memories is a slow process. Try to let it begin today. I pray for this gift for you. May you find peace in the present by being released from the past.

☙ **HEAVENLY FATHER**, the healing of hurtful memories is a long and delicate process. In them we relive the past with all its pain renewed in our minds and hearts. Come into the painful situations which I experienced in my life which still hurt, and gradually teach me how to forgive as your Son Jesus did. I feel guilty about my lack of forgiveness instead of admitting how deeply hurt I am, and how I need your help before I can walk on the road to forgiveness and reconciliation. Remove my feelings of guilt as you peel away the bandages of my wounds into which you pour your healing oil of mercy and forgiveness.

Now for the Good News

I am seventy-three years of age. My husband died three years ago and since then I have come into the Catholic Church after knowing for most of my life that this is where, deep in my heart, I wanted to be. As a young person I wanted to receive instruction, but my father would not hear of it. My parents were very good living and faithful to their Church which was Church of England.

During the War I met Peggy, a bombed-out friend who lived with us for three months. She was a Catholic. I started cycling with her to Mass and there we became friends with a wonderful priest. My husband whom I married in a C of E church was totally against him or any clergyman. It made for a very difficult marriage and I felt that with God's help I would get into the Church on my deathbed, but you see the Lord is good.

When my husband died I took instruction and became a Catholic. Now I can please myself and have found such peace. I can attend Mass and receive the Blessed Sacrament with no trouble. It has been a long wait but it has been well worth while.

MAUREEN

❦ **HOLY SPIRIT**, you give us people at various stages in our lives who bring us closer to you and to a fuller realisation of ourselves. I thank you for all those who awakened in me the beauty of my Christian faith. I pray for many of them who have long since gone to their reward. They would be amazed to learn what passed from their faith into mine without their ever knowing it. I am in large measure what they made me. I pray for my parents, family, school teachers, priests and nuns and the many others whose memory I carry and treasure in my life. May I pass on to others what I have received from them.

Our marriage is in a rut

Married for 12 years and still only 30 years old, our marriage has got into a rut. I still love my husband but I feel like a prisoner. We do the same thing week in week out with never anything different. I feel stifled. Why?

JUDITH

Life was never meant to be boring. Each day has fresh challenges to keep us alive and help us to look on life as an adventure. Life is boring if we are buried in a rut long before we physically die. A rut is always deeper than a grave because you are dead in a grave and know nothing of what is going on around you. In a rut you know there is life somewhere out there but you are not part of it.

May I suggest you write down the things you would like to do and share with your husband. Also look at your own interests before you married and see if you cannot take them up again. Sit down with your husband and discuss what you have written. Beforehand, please don't forget to say a prayer for patience, guidance and the gifts of courage and listening. I hope you will come out of the rut before it becomes the grave of your marriage. Don't die before your time.

❦ **LORD JESUS**, you saw life as a challenge. This is why you called Peter and the others to leave everything behind them and follow you. It is the same with marriage. A man and woman leave their homes to live together in marriage. Sometimes, because of many personality factors, and a dulling of their vision as to what marriage is all about, they lose their way and their life together becomes meaningless. Lord, help all married couples to pray for a renewal of their marriage ideals as they recapture their vision of what their life together should be.

I want to be popular

I crave acceptance by others. I want to be popular and so I say things to people which I know will please them. I know it is all so superficial and wrong. I never have the courage to stand up for my beliefs. What should I do?

BERNARD

No one wants enemies and you would be a very strange person indeed if you deliberately set out to make people dislike you. We all want to be accepted. Christ was like that except when he was forced to take issue with those who opposed his mission and teaching because of their prejudice and hatred.

Our first human inclination is to be friendly towards people. This, however, has its limits. There will come times when we have to stand up and be counted for what we hold dear in life. If we chicken out, and fail because of our lack of courage, then we are diminished in our own estimation and in that of discerning people.

We need to be liked or appreciated for who we are and what we stand for. The Christian faith has never been popular. When the Church tries to be popular, then it fails to deliver its full message.

Bernard, be true to yourself and then you can be false to no one. If people don't like you as you are, then they are the losers. Be someone whom your friends love and your 'enemies' respect. This is the only real acceptance worth having.

❦ **LORD JESUS**, you were loved by vast numbers of people who followed you everywhere even out into the desert. You did not court popularity, nor were you ever afraid to stand up and be counted for your beliefs and vision. The people saw in you someone whose actions fitted his words perfectly. Give me the courage and integrity of purpose to model my life on yours. May I never seek the easy way out of a difficult situation or be afraid to witness on behalf of others without undice concern for the consequences to myself. Help me to be true to you: then I cannot be false to anyone, including myself.

It is my last Christmas

I am thirty-four years old with four lovely children, the eldest ten and the youngest two years old. I have terminal cancer, and the doctors give me just three months to live. Pray that I will bear up this Christmas for the sake of my husband and children.

SUZANNE

It is not going to be easy for you or your husband. The knowledge that this may be your last Christmas together is a threat. You will have to face up to it. You will need all the faith and courage you can muster if you are really going to cope. My advice to you is given in what I hope is compassion and understanding.

Live this Christmas, Suzanne, as you have lived all your other Christmases together. Enjoy the fun and preparation with the children. This is going to be the best and most special Christmas of all. Let everything be as personal as possible. Choose your gifts with all the love you always did. They are part of you and your love for your husband and children.

Tell the children you love them and what a blessing they are. Let your laughter flow without any mixture of sorrow. At Christmastime the magic of love is in the air. Breathe it in and enjoy every moment. You and your husband have helped to make it. It will be a precious memory for your children which nothing or no one will ever take from them.

Doctors can be wrong. I know that. I pray, Suzanne, for your healing. It is God alone who decides when it is your last Christmas. Hang on to life by your finger nails. Never let go. I shall be thinking of you this Christmas and of others like you. You are in my love and prayers. You will cope because God will be with you.

❧ FATHER, you make us young again at Christmas when we thrill to the wonder of the birth of your Son. The magic of love is in the air which lifts us up and warms us in the cold bleakness of winter. It is a time to make us hope again. You are never far away from us in all our needs, and will not be outdone in generosity since you gave us your Son as a baby to be one of our family. Help me, Lord, this Christmas to think of life, love and happiness as I share in the celebration of the birth of Jesus your Son with those whom you have given me as my family.

Now for the Good News

I hope my letter will help people not to be frightened of cancer. Here is my story. My husband died very suddenly in 1971. We had no children, and I myself was the only child of parents

133

long since dead. In December 1971, I developed breast cancer and had my right breast removed.

Ten years later, I developed stomach cancer, and had half my stomach removed. I was very ill indeed and was given four to five months to live. I told my doctor, who was a very caring Catholic, that I was going to make the most of my life, and live every minute of those remaining months. From about a week after that I began to eat again and eventually to enjoy eating.

In 1983 I developed cancer on my back and had radium treatment. I have been extremely well since them.

I lead a very full active life. I help at my local cancer shop at least two four-hour shifts each week. I help for about half an hour weekly cleaning our local parish church. I go on rambles and day trips, and recently I had two day trips to France and Brussels. I play bridge twice weekly, and do all my own cooking and housework. In fact I have more bother with arthritis than anything else.

I take each day as it comes, but never forget to thank God every day for another day, and each morning for another night. I am in my eighty-sixth year, and I know that life is very precious and worth living. We should not meet trouble halfway. Let it do all the walking. I lead life to the full because I leave the future in God's gentle hands.

DORIS

❦ JESUS THE HEALER, nothing is impossible to you, and no situation is beyond your healing power. I praise you for all the times in my life when you healed me of my physical, emotional and spiritual pain. Your healing changed my life, and through it I came to an awareness of your love and compassion. I thank you for all those who have been healed by you in the past, and now witness to your holy name. Put into the hearts of those who suffer pain which seems never-ending, that you are the Lord of all, and by your love you heal in your own way, those who come to you in confident hope and trust.

Further Material on Healing

Books on Healing by Monsignor Michael Buckley

His Healing Touch   (Fount)
Christian Healing   (Catholic Truth Society)
Stories That Heal   (Darton, Longman and Todd)
More Stories That Heal   (Darton, Longman and Todd)
Treasury of the Holy Spirit (Hodder and Stoughton)
Let Peace Disturb You   (St Paul Publications)
Do Not Be Afraid   (Darton, Longman and Todd)

Tapes

1. *Healing the Person and God Our Healing Father*
2. *Healing and Suffering and the Healing Community*
3. *Healing in the Parish* (Canon Jimmy Collins)
   The El Shaddai Ministry (Oonagh Watters)
4. *The Peace of Christ and I Believe in Healing*
5. *The Healing of Fear and the Healing of False Guilt*
6. *Healing is Loving Yourself*
7. *Praying for Healing*
8. *Healing Brings Hope and Joy*
   Trusting God

All tapes except Tape 3 are by Monsignor Michael Buckley

For further information contact:
    'El Shaddai'
    9 West Ridings
    East Preston
    West Sussex
    BN16 2TD